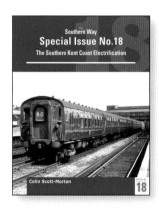

THE SOUTHERN WAY SPECIAL
Issue No 18
The Southern Kent Coast Electrification
ISBN 9781800350229
available in November 2021 at £16.95

To receive your copy the moment it is released, order in advance from your usual supplier, or it can be sent post-free (UK) direct from the publisher:

Crécy Publishing Ltd (Noodle Books)

1a Ringway Trading Estate, Shadowmoss Road, Manchester M22 5LH

Tel 0161 499 0024

www.crecy.co.uk

enquiries@crecy.co.uk

Acknowledgements

Few persons were around who actually witnessed the oil-burning engines when I commenced this research, and basically no one with first-hand knowledge. 'Anno Domini' and all that. Even so, we are fortunate to have two first-hand accounts previously recorded, firstly by George Blakey and the second by Hugh Abbinnett. Without these men's actual footplate experiences what follows would be almost totally based on fact rather than practical experience. In more recent times, I am most grateful to those individuals who have been prepared to dig deep into their own archives and collections, finding material that had likely laid dormant for years and which may now all be pulled together. In alphabetical order: Robin Fell at the Transport Treasury, Mike King, Gerry Nichols and the archives of the Stephenson Locomotive Society, David Postle at Kidderminster Railway Museum, Peter Swift, Andrew Royle also at Transport Treasury and Ian Wilkins. Several photographers whose work have been used are acknowledged individually.

Finally, one person deserves a special mention. This is David Lawrence, who resolutely worked away at various archives on my behalf finding material that I had honestly thought impossible to extricate. I owe him much.

'T9' No. 731 almost certainly at Eastleigh and probably soon after conversion. At this stage, generator and electric lights have still to be fitted. John Bailey's notes indicate that on 4 September he observed this engine in the converted state seen but on trial and 'about to be converted' 'L11' No. 437, and 'T9s' Nos 280, 314, and 713, together with 'Oil Pump No. 2', aka '701S' 'D1' No. 2284.

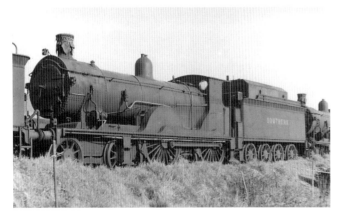

The type of image most associated with the oil-burning story; that of a stored engine awaiting its fate on 3 March 1951. Seen is 'T9' No. 118 stored at Fratton – notice the sacking tied around the chimney – along with two of its converted classmates. (We can identify the engine of the left as being an oil burner from the glimpse of the tubular alder on the rear of the tender.) At this stage No. 118 would have been stored since October 1948, not necessarily always at Fratton but it appears here and at Eastleigh were two storage depots. (There would be little point in moving them around anyway.) Despite having been out of use for twenty-nine months, it was still notionally 'on the books'. However, that would change with official withdrawal in April 1951 and it was finally dispatched in May 1951. Even at this stage of prolonged storage, the steam generator for the electric lighting (on the side of the smokebox) remains intact, as do the electric lights themselves. Indeed, it appears no stripping for spares of any parts has taken place. *Bluebell Railway Museum*

The Southern Way

Kevin Robertson

The Southern Railway Oil-Burning Engines: 1946-1951

Special Issue 17

www.crecy.co.uk

© 2020 Kevin Robertson

ISBN 9781910809709

First published in 2020 by Noodle Books

New contact details
All editorial submissions to:
The Southern Way (Kevin Robertson)
'Silmaril'
Upper Lambourn
Hungerford
Berkshire RG17 8QR
Tel: 01488 674143
editorial@thesouthernway.co.uk

A CIP record for this book is available from the British Library.

Publisher's note: Every effort has been made to identify and correctly attribute photographic credits. Any error that may have occurred is entirely unintentional.

Printed in Malta by Gutenberg

Noodle Books is an imprint of
Crécy Publishing Limited
1a Ringway Trading Estate
Shadowmoss Road
Manchester M22 5LH

www.crecy.co.uk

Front cover:
'T9' No. 113 outside the front of Eastleigh Works. probably soon after conversion to oil in September 1947. At least two members of the class, Nos 113 and 280. were repainted at or around the same time as the oil conversion, as were 'L11s' Nos 148, 155, and 437, 'D15' No. 463, and 'N' 1831. Otherwise the conversions emerged in the same external condition as when they entered works. It is likely this view may have been taken on 19 September 1947, on which date three other converted engines, Nos 314 ('T9'), 713 ('N15') and 722 ('N15') were also observed either at the Works or at the adjacent motive power depot. (All four engines were converted in the same month.) Dependent also on one's viewpoint, the conversions were either a fiasco by government or a wasted opportunity. *S.C. Nash/Stephenson Locomotive Society*

Rear cover:
Seven named engines were converted to burn oil between 1946 and 1948, including five members of the Urie 'N15' (better known as the 'King Arthur') class. Here No. 745 *Tintagel* appears to be receiving its final attention outside the front of Eastleigh shed prior to taking up its booked duty on 4 September 1948. The 1,600-gallon oil tank was located in the coal space, hence there was no loss of water capacity. Notice the way the top sides of the oil tank are tapered to conform with the loading gauge. Careful examination also reveals the tool box lid is open on the tender footplate. Electric lighting is also fitted. No. 745 ran in this condition from October 1947 until October 1948 and was then stored until reconverted back to coal in December 1948. *Mike King collection*

Title page:
An unidentified oil-burning 'T9' in charge of the Portsmouth portion of a through train from Brighton to Salisbury. The two sections will join at Fareham and continue via Southampton. The service is seen crossing the viaduct at Fareham and will shortly arrive at the station of the same name. Views of the oil burners in service are limited, and this shortage is not helped, of course, that we are looking at a very restricted timespan and it was also during a period when film was still not always easy to obtain. Few of these 'moving train' images also display much in the way of a visible exhaust from the chimney, such as here where the reason is one of three potential scenarios: good combustion, the burner and steam supply were both set at a very low volume, or both were in fact tuned off. Any one of the three might apply to this service as the train would be slowing for the Fareham stop. Relighting (in most cases) was by the simple expedient of tuning on both the steam and oil supply, which would cause the droplets of oil to vaporise in the heat of the firebox and simultaneously burst into flame. *Denis Callender*

Introduction

It is a fact of life that on occasions recent history can be more difficult to unravel than that of long ago. Records and files can be disposed of as being of no consequence, so leaving just a few bland entries in a minute book or contemporary journal. This would certainly appear to have been the case relative to the subject now under discussion.

In the course of collecting and compiling material for *Southern Way*, there have been a number of occasions when odd images of the Southern Railway oil-burning engines from the period have appeared on my desk. Most appeared to be stationary scenes and, while like most, I was aware of the bare bones of the story, I had absolutely no idea what a fascinating tale would unravel with 'a bit of digging'. Consequently, what I thought at the time would one day be a short photo insertion into a regular issue of *SW* has instead become what you now have before you.

Some students of the Southern will already be aware of the earlier oil-burning conversions of the SECR and SR. I have made the deliberate decision not to include details of these in this work and for two reasons. Firstly, I have nothing much further to add compared with that already published, and secondly, we already have more than sufficient material to fill this 'Special' issue – and I suspect the publisher has probably had enough of me 'over-delivering' on another book earlier this year! Consequently, so far as the earlier conversions are concerned I would recommend the reader refer to the late H. Holcroft's books *Locomotive Adventure* (Ian Allan, 1964 and 1965), Part 2 in particular, and which relevant piece has been reproduced in *Southern Way 51* for July 2020.

Reverting back to my comments about attempting to unravel recent history, it appears the whole oil burning story of 1946–51 is contained within a number of files deposited at the National Archives (Kew) and it is from these that the majority of information that follows was gleaned. No doubt Eastleigh (and Fratton) especially also retained their own files on the practicalities of the conversions as well as day-to-day operations and these may well have been once accessible to that doyen of researchers D.L. Bradley at the time he was gathering information for what would later appear as his *History of the Locomotives of the SECR/LSWR/Southern*, etc.

Bradley, though was constrained, not just by space in his eventually published books but likely also by how much he could copy on his visits to Eastleigh. (We know that during a number of official shed visits in which he participated he would often 'absence' himself, reappearing later having no doubt found another hoard of dusty files.)

As I have oft quoted in the past, it is a great pity these 'day-to-day' ('operational' might be a better term) files have not survived. That they existed we can have no doubt. As an example, when Bulleid asks (or is asked) questions, the answers appear in the National Archive correspondence, so we know other paperwork existed locally.

We should also not forget that the period in question especially the years 1946–48 were far from easy, both for the Southern Railway and the country in general. Wartime shortages and in consequence rationing was still in place, the winter of 1947 was especially difficult and, while not to put too fine a point on it, the country was also broke. Here most will know the story from this point on; the belief that by converting engines to burn oil it would save on coal usage, which in turn may then be sold overseas to gain valuable foreign currency and so enable the country to buy goods that were essential but which we were unable to make ourselves. And then, of course, the government realised we did not have enough foreign currency to purchase the oil needed in the first place.

That will be the story known to most. It is mostly true but with an awful lot of caveats and twists and turns along the way.

It has been a fascinating tale to unravel and we almost managed to find an image of every one of the conversions, due to the wonderful help I have received from friends, archives libraries and 'other sources'. I sincerely hope you will enjoy the results.

Kevin Robertson
Berkshire 2020

1
We must all do as we are bidden

Publicly the first inkling of oil burning on the railways (and here and as on occasions elsewhere there are times when for the sake of completeness we have to mention railways other than the Southern), is contained within the pages of the *Railway Magazine* for November/December 1946, where on p.376 commences a general two-page article 'Oil Fuel on British Railways'. The article starts, 'The statement by the Minister of Transport at the end of August that he had authorised the main-line railway companies to proceed as quickly as possible with the conversion of 1,217 locomotives from coal to oil burning has directed attention once again to a method of fitting widely used abroad, but which has never been adopted in this country wither extensively, or for any lengthy period.'

The piece continued, without illustrations, to describe the previous oil-fired experiments on the various British railways but with no further mention of what was now proposed. Instead it was left to a perhaps unlikely source to afford more detail. This was the *Meccano Magazine* simultaneously in its own issue of November 1946 within the regular 'Railway Notes' feature, which provides for an interesting aside on the intended

Senior officers from the four railway companies made up the Railway Executive Committee (REC), seen here at 'Battle HQ' during the Second World War, which was, as we know, also the first time oil firing had been discussed. They are L to R: Eustace Missenden (SR), James Milne (GWR, William Wood (LMS), unknown, E.G. Marsden (Secretary), Charles Newton (LNER), Frank Pick (LPTB), Ralph Wedgwood (LNER), unknown, V.M. Barrington Ward.

conversions to take place on both the Southern and the other railways. Dealing first with the Southern (naturally), the figure was for 100 engines to be converted; on the LMS the figure was 485 engines including all the S&D 2-8-0 engines (of which more anon), the thirty-three Beyer-Garratt type and five 'Class 5s'. On the LNER it was intended that just freight types would burn oil, the largest number from a single class being 111 of the Riddles design 'Austerity' 2-8-0s. The figure for the GWR was 198 and, as with the SR, an altogether more eclectic mix consisting of fifty of the 'Castle' class, 85 'Hall' class, and sixty-three '28xx/38xx' locos – see table at the end of this chapter.

The technical journal *The Railway Gazette* appears to have made three references to oil burning, on 18 January, 16 August and again on 30 August 1946. All three were subsequently combined by the same publisher into a booklet entitled *Conversion of Locomotives from Coal to Oil Burning* and released some time later in the same year. We know that the 18 January entry had referred to the experiences of the GWR with the first conversions of their 28xx type 2-8-0 locomotives and meaning oil firing on the GWR had commenced in the previous year. As such it is very difficult and also inappropriate to attempt to look at the SR venture unilaterally and there are times such as now when a multilateral approach is necessary. (*The Railway Pictorial and Locomotive Review Vol. 1* for 1946 also includes a brief mention but without the detail of the other publications mentioned.)

Arguably the most useful information contained within the *Railway Gazette* pamphlet is the first page alone, after which the remaining pages are devoted to the conversion and operation of the converted GWR 2-8-0 engine. It is therefore appropriate to start with that first page in its entirety:

> 'At the end of August, the Minister of Transport, Mr Alfred Barnes, issues a statement indicating that he had authorised the main-line railway companies to proceed as quickly as possible with the conversion of 1,217 locomotives from coal to oil burning, in order to secure a saving of coal estimated at 20,000 tons a week or approximately 1,000,000 tons per annum. The three main featured of the scheme are the alteration of the engines by providing oil-burning equipment; the supply and erection of oil storage installations in the locomotive depots at some 58 places; and the construction of some hundreds of tank wagons for transporting the oil from the ports to the storage depots.'

The article continues further but for the present we need to stop and analyse some of the statements already made. So, it seems the whole was now already authorised, which means there must have been previous discussion.

We can trace this back into one general and one specific area. The first is that during the Second World War, by inference around 1942, plans had already been formulated to convert locomotives to oil. Whether this related to the period in question or was a plan for post-war development is not certain. Considering the actual time the post-war timescale would certainly seem the more likely.

We also know that during the war there were a number of committees at which various senior officers of the 'Big Four' and London Transport met. One of these involved the General Managers' and upon which sat Missenden for the SR, Milne for the GWR, Wood for the LMS Wood, Newton for the LNER, and Pick for the LPTB. Secretary to the group was E.G. Marsden; title and railway/civil service position not reported. Others from the respective companies with specific expertise might join some meetings according to need.

One other committee relevant to the discussion was that of the Railway Executive Mechanical and Electrical Engineers' Committee. Bulleid sat on this representing the Southern and according to John Click (a former Bulleid pupil), 'I think OVB hated committees unless he was the Chairman, and wasn't keen even then.'

We might be expected to think that individuals in the same senior positions on their respective railways would be succinct in their thoughts and deliberate in their decisions. Not perhaps quite so according to R.G. Jarvis when referring to the period 1942–44. Stanier, by then Sir William, was Chairman and Jarvis looked after his papers. Thompson was there from the LNER (and, as R.C. Bond once observed, with his array of gold pens and pencils at the ready), plus the Chief Mechanical Engineer (CME) of the Great Western, Hawksworth and Bulleid was also present with his Electrical Engineer, Raworth.

'OVB was rather whimpering, which may surprise you, but not really. Instead he was something of a prima donna, happier leading rather than listening. Earlier at this same Committee he had been decisive enough when an urgent call for a thousand wagons for Persia had come up. Asked what they could do, the other CMEs volunteered small numbers of different wagon types which they proposed to "sole and heel", whereupon OVB said he knew exactly what people out there needed: only one type of new wagon. "With a bit of help we will build them in the time at Ashford." Shop 40 (known locally as the "madhouse") did him proud "and," Bulleid told me, "all the wagons got there".'

So we know that at some stage oil-firing had been mentioned at least during the Second World War, while the first confirmed mention of it for the Southern appears in a note from RMT Richards, the Traffic Manager of the Southern, who in a memo of 20 November 1945 reporting a conversation between himself and Bulleid, suggests discussion had taken place on the conversion of ten members of the 'Q1' class to burn oil. Nothing else is heard on this proposal.

Elsewhere in his memoirs, Click informs us Bulleid was keen on the idea of oil firing – strange then he appears not to have picked up on the idea with the 'Q1' – and this might even have been when his mind turned towards incorporating this type of fuel in what eventually developed into his 'Leader' design.

We must now turn away slightly in the direct of Swindon/Paddington, where we can report that the GWR were themselves becoming concerned over the availability of locomotive coal in 1946. Whether this was actually in that year or not is not reported but from what follows it would seem likely to have arisen in late 1945 at least. Why the concern? Well, put simply, the government had decreed that the best

'Q1' 0-6-0 No. C18. The conversion of ten members of the 'Q1' class to burn oil was referred to as having taken place in a conversation between the Southern Railway Traffic Manager, Mr R.M.T. Richards and the Chief Mechanical Engineer Mr O.V.S. Bulleid around November 1945. Nothing else came of, or was heard of, the proposal or bunkering facilities, and converting any of the type is certainly not mentioned when the 1946–47 list was prepared of engines to burn oil. Had this gone ahead in 1945 then there was every chance the Southern Railway may have equalled or even beaten the GWR with a unilateral oil fuel programme.

Welsh coal be sent for export – again the importance of foreign currency comes to the fore – and instead the country was importing inferior-grade fuel with the seemingly ridiculous scenario that locomotives were failing through shortage of steam in, of all places, south Wales!

Although hardly reported much since in the railway press, it is also reported that some steam-hauled services were having extra time built into their schedules to allow for stop(s) en route to allow for fire cleaning to take place. This was certainly the case on the Southern and if one company was affected it must surely be very likely that the others were as well. The fuel on offer was of such poor state that clinkering of the firebars was a regular problem. We, of course, know the railways were in a poor state generally post-war, arrears of maintenance alone resulting in reduced speeds and associated longer journey times. Add into the mix the necessary time for fire cleaning and it became clear to see how, to the public at least, the steam engine was deemed to be outmoded. It was a belief that was hardly fair but easy to understand.

Consequently, in its own independent fashion the decision was made by Swindon/ Paddington to experiment with oil fuel and the GWR were able to report that on 6 June 1946 they already had twelve locomotives converted to burn oil with another thirty-two to follow. Whether these numbers are accurate and what the engines were – and where based – is detail not relevant to the present text.

But what is relevant is the GWR comment, again mixed up in the National Archives paperwork, is that Swindon/Paddington were becoming increasingly concerned about the availability of coal supplies for the coming winter. This was a highly important point as well for it should be recalled that at this period in time Britain was a nation and an industry that was primarily fuelled on coal and with demand especially in the domestic market likely to increase in the winter months.

The Southern and likely also the other companies were quick to take note and the official paperwork refers to the Southern liaising with the GWR, with the latter agreeing to provide details of their conversions.

It was most likely the Minister of Transport who became aware of the conversions and its seeming success through the Railway Executive Mechanical and Electrical Engineers' Committee, and this in turn would have been fed back to other government departments including those responsible for fuel. In consequence, we learn the government then started discussion with other (unspecified) industries that might themselves convert to oil instead of coal, which in turn would so release coal stocks and so on.

We should mention that, unlike GWR plans of years before where coal-burning locomotives would have failed to operate in areas west of Taunton (this was a scheme considered and then abandoned by the GWR in the inter-war years), this time it was not just one area that would be converted and the scheme envisaged oil burning in several areas concurrently.

Meanwhile, we are given details of the amount of ordinary diesel oil being used as a fuel by the four railway companies and calculated (in tons rather than gallons) just on the basis of the number of diesel shunters operated by the railways.

One could very well summarise the whole oil burning episode in these two images of 'D15' No. 463, and similarly with the words 'hope and despair'. In the first view we see the engine at Eastleigh soon after conversion (September 1947) but before the addition of electric lights (fitted by the end of 1947). In the second image she is dumped at Eastleigh on 26 May 1951 and yet not officially withdrawn until November some months after all the other converted 4-4-0s had been reduced to nothing. As an oil burner, No. 463 was reported as a good performer and worked certain of the Waterloo–Bournemouth services. All ten of the class had been intended to be converted but the scheme was stopped before progressing beyond No. 463. *W. Gilburt/R.K. Blencowe and Tony Sedgwick*

GWR: One diesel using 30 tons of fuel per year.

LMS: Forty diesel locomotives using 2,250 tons per year.

LNER: Four diesel locomotives using 250 tons per year.

SR: Four diesel locomotives using 300 tons per year.

Note the diesel railcars operated by the GWR are not for whatever reason included in the figure, the most likely explanation for this omission being there was nothing in the other companies to compare them against. The discrepancy between fuel usage for the same number of engines between the LNER and SR is also not explained; perhaps on one system it was simply a case of the engines having more work required of them.

There is no mention anywhere of fuel supplies being an issue for these engines (and the railcars), while evidence presented by the GWR also showed that oil could well have an advantage as the best Welsh coal had a calorific value of 14,000Btu whereas oil fuel supplied by the Anglo-Iranian Oil Company produced 18,000Btu. This was all very well but what no one seems to have taken into account was that on 21 August 1946 good-quality coal was costing £2 10s per ton; oil on the other hand was £7 1s per ton. Again, using the GWR as an example, average coal consumption had increased by slightly more than 20 per cent per engine mile in the five years 1939 to 1944, accounted by the quality of coal decreasing and more delays en route. We could no doubt apply a similar situation to the other companies. The *Railway Gazette* picked up on this cost differential – it was hard to ignore it – but assumed (it did *not* confirm) that the additional cost would be borne by the government. A similar statement was made over the actual costs of the depot installations.

Even so, and seemingly discarding the cost differential, the government were convinced of the benefits of oil and a formal notice was issued to the railway companies on 31 July 1946 that it was proposed to reduce the amount coal available to them by 20,000 tons per week from 1 January 1947. Oil fuel would instead be used. It gave the 'Big Four' just five months to design, install, test and have the oil operation up and running. (According to O.S. Nock in his work *The British Steam Locomotive 1925–1965 Vol. 2*, p.190 and 195, the success of the GW project, albeit at the time on a limited scale, had led the government of the day to

embark on a nationwide scheme for oil firing. The GWR policy conceived as intended to be a long-term feature of steam locomotive operation.)

So, with 1,217 engines to convert, perhaps the Great Western was thus fortunate in having already started, but as we will see much later, that advantage would turn into an eventual disadvantage.

For the sake of completeness the conversion programme then envisaged was as follows:

	Class of Loco	Number to be converted	Total	Actual conversions
GWR	28xx	63		
	49xx	84		
	Castle	25		
			172	
LNER	04	112		
	01	39		
	WD Austerity	111		
	K3	91		
	Q6	46		
	J39	35		
	02	16		
			450	
LMSR	Beyer-Garratt	33		
	Class 7 0-8-0	175		
	Class 8 2-8-0	266		
	S&D 2-8-0	11		
			485	
SR	West Country	20		1 +1 *see* p.74 and 83
	N15/H15	16		6 × N15
	N & U	34		1 × N, 2 × U
	D15	10		1
	L11/T9	30	110	8 × L11, 13 × T9
Totals			1217	33

The above comes from the first page of the *Railway Gazette* pamphlet already spoken of. It was also a 'first' list, although we also do not know of any others! The reason for referring to it as such is simply that on the SR at least the engine types selected did change slightly and consequently changes may also have been made to the proposals from the other companies as well; we know, for example, that the GWR were also considering the conversion of some of their 42xx/52xx 2-8-0T class at one time.

At one point, the term 'Pacific locos' was used without differential as to whether these might be of the 'Merchant Navy' or 'West Country' type. Clearly, the *Railway Gazette* had resolved this, at least for their publication.

The same *Railway Gazette* page gives information on the locomotive depots to be equipped for oil fuel. These totalled fifty-eight, and again for completeness were as follows:

GWR: Old Oak Common, Reading, Didcot, Swindon, Bristol St Phillips Marsh and Bath Road, Newton Abbot, Plymouth (Laira), Severn Tunnel Junction, Ebbw Junction, Newport, Cardiff, Landore, Gloucester, Westbury and Banbury.

LNER: March, Hansey, Peterborough, Doncaster, Gorton, Mexborough, Darnell, Heaton, Newport Tyneside, Carlisle, St Margaret's Edinburgh, Cowlairs, Stratford and Darlington.

LMSR: Cricklewood, Toton, Westhouses, Staveley, Hasland, Carlisle, Leeds, Normanton, Nottingham, Kirkby, Willesden, Bath, Crewe, Wakefield, Farnley Junction, Newton Heath, Aintree, Shrewsbury, Swansea, Wellingborough, Lostock Hall, Northampton, Nuneaton, Rose Grove and Mirfield.

SR: Eastleigh, Fratton, Exmouth Junction.

The aim of the conversions was, of course, to save coal but as we know, in reality the whole episode achieved little. Certainly some passenger and freight services were operated by the oil-fired engines, with one example seen here, 'T9' No. 113 in charge of a Portsmouth–Bristol service made up of GWR coaching stock and recorded passing Millbrook, west of Southampton sometime in 1947. *S.C. Townroe/R.K. Blencowe*

Right: **Taken from the 1947 R.J. Eaton pamphlet, the list of proposed depot conversions is shown. Some changes were later made in the proposed locations; Ebbw Junction, for example, not being included on the map.**

All this was fine in theory but it must also be recalled that materials in general were in short supply, although the small print of the government announcement included that the Ministry of Supply 'has given every possible assistance in the provision of the material necessary for equipment and storage tanks'. Some standardisation was also envisaged but this was more in the form of parts rather than complete installations, while individual engine types meant there could not be standardisation in every area. The announcement also referred to the type but not the number of tank wagons that would be required to carry fuel from the port unloading points to the rail depots, stating that these tank cars would require steam heating coils to be fitted.

The GWR was held up to high account by the government for its pioneering work, while the announcement also referred to a possible temporary disruption of services both as locomotives were temporarily withdrawn for conversion but also as men were taken off repair and overhaul work and moved to across to deal with the conversions.

Interestingly, a memo exists in the official files from an unnamed but clearly both experienced and farsighted individual who comments, 'Heavy duty locos which consume the most

amount of fuel will be selected. It will be interesting to see if the claim that they will be smokeless or almost smokeless when running will be justified in practice. I have vivid memories of oily black smoke that belched from chimneys in the emergency periods of 1921 and 1926 and comparable perhaps with the inferior coal of recent years which has itself been an unwelcome cause of smoky lineside experiences.'

'An impossible ask'

There was a fraction over four months then from the end of August to the end of December 1946 for the Southern to plan and execute government instructions. Could it be done in time, would both depots and locomotives be ready and could staff in turn be instructed on the use of the fuelling facilities and the locomotives?

In reality the answer in all cases was an understandable and emphatic 'No', this single statement coming as early as 15 August 1946 from Mr V.A.M. Robertson, the Chief Civil Engineer (CCE) of the Southern, who commented it was impossible to have the Motive Power depots up and running by the General Manager's (and in reality the government's) requested target date of 1 January 1947 Indeed, some time later Mr Robertson was fulsome in his comments as to how many draughtsmen he had been forced to reallocate to the scheme and at the same time how many others projects were delayed (*see* p.45).

As previously mentioned, future conversion to oil fuel had first been mooted in the Second World War. It is thus reasonable to assume that at that time some plans would have been drawn up, certainly so far as the locomotive issues were concerned, and decisions made appertaining to fuelling facilities – on the SR that is. Again whether such decisions were shared or whether each company would 'go it alone' is not reported, certainly we know the government would have preferred a common approach. The Southern had some advantage, along with the LNER (courtesy of the GE and GCR oil-burning engines of some decades before) with their own oil firing in LSWR and early SR days. I think it also fair to say such paperwork as existed from those times would have been dusted down and referred to now.

Why the government figure of 1,217 engines was chosen is not known, although presumably it would have been left to the individual companies to make their own choices. With hindsight, too, it would surely have made more sense to concentrate efforts (this is every company) at just one or possible a maximum of two depots. That way experience could have been gained should a larger programme be rolled out sometime later in the future.

Moving away now from 'unhappy bunnies', we instead turn to one of the two anomalies specific to oil burning (the terms 'oil burning' and 'oil firing' are used turn and turnabout in the present text and should be read as meaning the same thing.) This was the August 1946 conversion of a 'Terrier' No. 515S.

This particular engine was at the time gainfully employed as one of the regular Lancing Works shunters but was taken into works to emerge converted to burn oil fuel. When and where, although presumably in the latter case at Brighton, and especially why is not recorded in any located official paperwork but a clue emerges from Bradley, who states this was, '... to give officials experience of oil-fired locomotives'. But who were these 'officials', surely a strange term that is not elaborated upon.

Of the eight SR locomotive classes from which examples were due to converted to burn oil, it was only the 'H15' that ended up with none being dealt with. Official paperwork simply refers to '16 × 4-6-0 N15/ H15' as being on the schedule, but how this number would have been divided is not explained. It is all the stranger because, as reported on 31 March 1947, it had been said that parts were to hand to convert one of the each of the SR types. Seen here is an example of the class, No. 30333 at Eastleigh (as a coal burner of course) on 28 March 1958. *Tony Molyneaux*

There are also innumerable other questions that we simply do not have answers for: what was the capacity of the oil tank on 515S; where and how was it refuelled; what type of burner was provided, etc? We know little else except to comment, and again from Bradley, there were difficulties in keeping the fire alight and that it continued its work in modified from in its previous role at Lancing until the end of 1946.

Tom Middlemas, author of *Stroudley and his Terriers*, now takes up the story with No. 515S back at work and still burning oil in February 1947. It remained at work in this guise until about August of the same year, when it was repainted black and reconverted to coal shortly afterwards, possibly in October 1947 – ironically while other engines were still being modified from coal to oil. As such it is probably fair to say No. 515S did little to promote the case for oil firing, although its unique claim fame remains as the only SR tank engine converted, indeed the only tank engine converted by the big four at the time. (We may exclude the 'D1' tank engines associated with oil pumping and which are referred to later as these, of course, remained coal fired.) No. 515S* is also not counted in the total of oil-fired engines on the SR.

0-6-0T No. 515IS in original coal-burning guise. No. 515S had been built in 1879 as No. 50 *Whitechapel*, and was converted to a member of the 'A1X' class in May 1920. Renumbered 650 in June 1901, it became B650 under Southern Railway ownership in 1923. Renumbered and named No. W9 *Fishbourne*, it was sent 'overseas' in May 1930, returning to the mainland in May 1936. It now languished at Eastleigh until re-emerging in April 1937 as No. 515S in the Departmental listing for shunting at Lancing. Under BR it retained its previous role, but now with the slightly modified identification of DS515. Renumbered into capital stock as No. 32650, it was one of the class that worked the Hayling Island branch until closure and consequent withdrawal in November 1963. It has been subsequently preserved – in its conventional coal-burning form.

The one that almost got away as there has been limited mention in published railway volumes of the involvement of No. 515S in the trials. Converted at Brighton in August 1946 and operating solely between Brighton and Lancing and then at Lancing Works, we do have to ask, exactly for what purpose was the engine changed to burn oil? Officially the reason given was to gain experience but on the basis of its mediocre performance, did it actual teach anything at all – perhaps except as showing 'how not to do it'! This is the only known image of the engine in its converted guise with a rectangular (at the top at least) oil tank in the bunker (we do not know the capacity), possibly around August 1946 and certainly recorded at Brighton with the fire alight. A large tool box would later be added to the top of the right-hand tank top similar to those carried on the tenders of most/all of the tender locomotives converted. Upon its reversion to coal, it retained this none too aesthetically pleasing embellishment. Electric lighting was not fitted. (The same type of substantial tool box was fitted to the top of the right-hand side tank of No. 32640 of the same class as well.) *Real Photographs R9314*

* The GWR had done slightly better with their publicity as an article on their own oil conversions appeared in their in-house *Great Western Magazine* in the autumn of 1945.

For comparison purposes only, here are two conventional 'Terriers' again at Lancing and both coal burning. What is interesting about the conversions of No. 515S is how it might have been bunkered and where? The LMS tender in the background is clearly a simple water carrier as there is no oil tank visible in the coal space but two similar LMS tenders were later at Eastleigh with oil tanks fitted.

So what might the Southern have learned from No. 515S, and who had authorised it and why? The answer to the first question is that it probably taught very little except that a small firebox was probably not ideal. As to whom authorised it, the present author's supposition – and with nothing more to go on that 'he liked the idea of oil fuel' – was Bulleid. After all, he was still very much in charge at Brighton at this time and similarly riding high on the popularity, and I suppose we should say success, of his Pacifics. We may conveniently ignore their occasional foibles.

The fact information on this aspect of history is so hard to find is unfortunate. Even the in-house *Southern Railway (Region) Magazine* seems to singularly fail to refer to the conversions in detail in any of its issues covering the period 1946 through to the end of 1948, although a veiled hint exists on p.183 of the September 1946* edition where, within a box emblazoned in bold type, are the words, The Fuel Problem is now VITAL. Save all we can, coal, gas, electricity'. The word 'vital' was printed in bold.) This was followed four pages later in the same issue with a reference to the 'Save Fuel' campaign having been inaugurated, with mention of demonstrations being given about how to stoke central heating and hot water boilers but without any mention of oil firing or locomotive conversions. Finally in the August 1947 issue on p.152, a single paragraph under the heading 'Oil Fuel Depot' appears as follows: 'As part of the national effort to conserve stocks of

coal, the Company is proceeding with schemes for the conversion of locomotives to oil burning. This necessitates the construction of oil-fuelling depots at various points and work has commenced on the installation of one at Exmouth Junction. It is hoped the plant will be working by the end of October.' There was no accompanying illustration or plan.

A similar gap exists reference official photographs. The Southern must have recorded these but with two exceptions where and in what archive (assuming they exist) has been impossible to ascertain. This might all sound defeatist, it is not intended to be, but instead just proves the point that while much has been uncovered, in so doing it has opened up areas where gaps still remain.

As if to prove this, we should note that just a single view of the converted 'Terrier' has been located, while apart from that already mentioned within the *Southern Railway Magazine,* its successor produced under British Railways in 1948 did marginally better by having an oil burner in the background of an unrelated image but even then without mentioning it in the caption.

Proof that discussions and planning had been going on behind the scenes prior to the government's public announcement of August 1946 comes from a set of minutes from the CME's Mechanical and Electrical Committee meeting of 2 July 1946, chaired by Bulleid.

The only two 'official'-type images located of the SR scheme; considered 'officials' as the background has been erased. Taken at the same time (notice the position of the engine valve gear), they show the first conversion 'N15' No. 740 *Merlin* in Southern livery. (Slightly tongue in cheek, but was there a sort of impish choice made in the selection of this engine with this name for the first SR choice (excluding 515S, of course)? We see the engine from front and rear and as yet without electric lighting. *Mike Morant and Jeremy Staines*

Here it is stated that the government had *indicated* (interesting, not confirmed), that 600,000 tons of heavy fuel oil ('Bunker 'C' type) would be available to industry per quarter and '... generally from the latter part of present year'. An 'appreciable proportion' of this could also be placed at the railway companies.

The M & E committee discussed this total, which represented 12,500 tons per week. Based on a consumption figure per loco per week of 20 tons, to utilise this amount 625 locos would need to be converted plus spare engines. (Presumably the figure of 20 tons came from contemporary GWR experience but this is not stated as such.) There is no mention of for what purpose the remaining 450,000 tons per annum would be used, but then again this was hardly the concern of the CMEs.

Allowing also for a two-week supply at each depot, this meant that the total railway storage capacity required was in the order of 25,000 tons. Taking into account engine usage, it equated to ten depots each with sixty engines. (These being

the figures minuted by the Committee.)

The next item discussed was costs and not surprisingly as these were CMEs it was the locomotive costs that come in for the most comment, indeed the depot costs are summarised in one brief sentence, 'Cost of ten depots without land £100,000.' The land comment taken to assume that the oil facilities would be built on existing railway land without the need for additional purchase.

So far as the locomotive conversions were concerned the conversion for oil burning was just under £1,000 per loco – £600,000 for the conversion of 625 engines. How this figure was arrived at – and presumably some loco types would be more expensive than others – is not explained. Yet again, proof we are missing some files. Consider also that these costs are 1946 figures, but they are the only ones we have and on the basis the majority of conversions actually occurred in the following year, 1947, we have no indication later as to whether they were actually kept to.

The cost of fitting 625 locos was estimated at £600,000 and it was decided that 1,500 men would be needed for the work. (This does somehow seem rather excessive, especially as it appears to refer solely to locomotive work – not forgetting the tenders, of course.)

It appears a consensus was reached shortly after between the government and the respective CMEs as there is an acknowledgement that the companies were unable to undertake all the necessary conversion work themselves without this having an adverse effect on existing repair and new build schedules. At this stage no mention is made of ground (installation/servicing) work. Looking back from seven decades later it is easy to see the 'chicken and egg' situation that was developing; the converted engines could not work without refuelling facilities, while conversely there was no point in having these without engines converted to use them.

So far as the locomotive conversions, most of the work involved firebox and tender alterations; the fitting of a burner into the firebox, a brick arch of different design and construction and the addition of firebricks to the firebox sides rising approximately one third to one half the height of the actual firebox. The firebricks were reported to be of the Alite 'D' type.

This in turn resulted in a reduction in grate area but this did not as it transpired adversely affect the ability to produce steam. The firebricks used both for the revised brick arch and for the firebox sides were also produced to a different (unspecified) composition.

The locomotive work would mainly be the province of boiler makers, which it was naturally stated would also react most unfavourably within the actual repair shops as there would now be an imbalance in the normal work they would undertake; again new build and repair. (Some loco classes had the benefit of having spare boilers, so this might have eased the situation initially at least.) Consequently, the CMEs were of the opinion that a maximum of ten locomotives per week could be dealt with (it was not specified if this meant 'per railway company' or 'in total').

Electric shunter at Durnsford Road (Wimbledon) and with the coal-fired railway power station in the background. This plant provided most (much) of the current for the South Western electrified network, supplemented when necessary from other sources. It was suggested that coal might be superseded by oil to fuel the boilers here but this was rejected. However, other static locations on the SR were also suggested but we have no evidence any were converted, either at the time or later. During the initial planning stage, Roland C. Bond (later CME of BR), at the time occupying a senior position on the LMS, sometimes deputised for his chief, H.G. Ivatt, on the M & E committee. In his autobiography, Bond recounts that firebox maintenance was higher with the oil burners but that the heat content of 68lb of oil was equal to 100lb of coal. At the then existing price (we may assume 1946–47) coal was 0.29d for lb and oil 0.81d, so fuel costs with oil were approximately two and a half times that of coal.

A figure of 500 extra men is also referred to (then, for the same task, 560 are mentioned), these having to come from outside sources. Again this is a figure that is hard to comprehend unless, as before, this is taking into account depot installation work as well. The CMEs were clearly less than keen on the prospect, regardless of whether oil might have been an improvement on the coal then available to them. They conclude a joint statement with the words, 'If the railways have to provide staff the result will be engines in shops for longer periods and fewer engines in service. The CMEs do not recommend the conversion of further locos and in their view greater advantage would be obtained at much less costs and loss of labour by conversion of central power stations.' By the word 'further' we may assume this meant outside of those already converted by the GWR as by this date certainly no other conversions, exception 515S, which is not mentioned anywhere else, had been modified.

E.G. Marsden wrote to the government outlining the position along the following lines, '... the number of conversions that could be effected would not have any material effect on coal position in coming winter'. But Whitehall were adamant that conversions were to take place and that coal savings from elsewhere other than the railways were impractical.

Before moving on, we might mention that comment is made on 9 September as to whether savings on coal might also be achieved in the power stations and boilers operated by the Southern Railway. These were referred as being the stationary boiler '... at the Waterloo & City railway station ...' and at 'Slades Green' depot, both suggested as to be considered to burn oil. A saving of 1,500 tons of coal p.a. might thus be achieved. Durnsford Road power station near Wimbledon was the other suggestion, the latter location where the SR generated power for much of its South Western lines third-rail network. An estimated conversion cost from coal to oil of £100,000 is mentioned but it is not clear if this was just the for last named or all three locations.

Certainly a first reaction is that Durnsford Road at least made obvious sense, at which point we have to ask from where did this/these conversion ideas emanate? The first reaction has to be the SR but it appears not, for the SR note the boilers at Durnsford Road were '... old and if converted would have to run at a reduced evaporation rate of 18,000lb per hour – it was not stated what the normal rate was. The SR also state that in the previous year, 1946, recourse had to be made to the London Electricity Supply Co. for additional power into the rail network. Clearly the government were becoming almost desperate to achieve the required savings as it must already have been abundantly clear there was no way the required numbers could be achieved in the limited timescale. Evidently the Southern's negative reaction to a possible conversion at Durnsford Road (and we believe fixed installations elsewhere) was enough to cancel this proposal. (It was reported later that a stationary boiler at Eastleigh Works was running on the same type of heavy oil, certainly by c.1948. Whether this was in fact a conversion from this timescale or a pre-existing situation is not known.)

We now retrace our steps slightly (with apologies, the whole story is full of points at which one could slip up – deliberate pun) to 30 July 1946 when Bulleid, as Chairman of the M & E Committee, referred in some detail to the required number of tank wagons that would be needed. (Historically it has always been tradition to refer to wagons carrying oil-based products as 'cars' rather than 'wagons', although the term was not applied to every liquid-carrying wagon; hence 'milk tanks'. For the purpose of this text vehicles carrying oil will be referred to as they were in contemporary reports.)

Bullied compared the number of locomotives it was deemed feasible to convert by the end of 1946 and with it the requisite number tank wagons that would be needed based on the perceived number of depot installations that it was then anticipated would be in operation:

Company	Locos anticipated as converted to burn oil commencing 1 October 1946	Number of tank wagons required	Anticipated saving in coal (tons)
GWR	16	100	3,000
LNER	20	300	6,800
LMS	21	325	8,000
SR	3	50	1,400

Exactly where Bulleid obtained these figures from is unknown but it was clearly with the knowledge and approval of his committee. However, surely even he must have seen it was all hopelessly optimistic. Reported at the end of July, could they really hope to have sixty engines converted *and* the requisite installations ready in just two months? We know Bulleid exaggerated slightly sometimes but surely even he must have seen it as an impossible ask. Perhaps instead we should read it as a holding statement, something to appease the government and when it failed, as it most certainly did, a message that what was being asked might then be sent to say it was just not feasible. As a further aside, we might also wonder how the GWR

had managed up to now so far as supplying their own converted engines and depots. (In response to this the reader is referred to the section within the book *The GWR Exposed* referred to in the bibliography.)

Notwithstanding any apparent reluctance on the part of individuals, committees or even a particular railway company, we know that progress, so far as planning/progress meetings was concerned, was rapid. Hence, on 7 August 1946 (still three weeks before the Minister's public announcement) a memorandum was sent from the Chief Mechanical Engineer's Office at Brighton to the General Manager at Waterloo giving for the first time details of the proposed SR ground installations.

These were to be at:

Eastleigh – capacity 400,000 gallons equivalent to 1,607 tons.

Exmouth Junction – 250,000 gallons, 1,004 tons

Fratton – 50,000 gallons, 201 tons. Here we also know the size of each storage tank as being 30ft × 9ft.

This was subject to the selected depots having suitable sites and each installation being practical so far as the Chief Civil Engineer was concerned with room for sufficient sidings that would not interfere with existing shed requirements. Site meetings were arranged at each as a matter of urgency.

The same paperwork then referred to the number of SR engines to be converted. A total of 110 was noted, with the number of oil-burning engines at each depot (but at this stage not broken down with full detail) as:

Eastleigh – 58

Exmouth Junction – 37

Fratton – 15

It was recognised that the converted engines would mean some adjustments to the engine diagrams, with the conversions intended to work both passenger and freight duties.

Discussion then turned to the practicalities of conversion and here it was said the maximum that it was possible to convert was ten per week (it was not stated if this would have involved all three SR loco works or just Eastleigh). But even so, ten conversions would still mean a general reduction of two major repairs/overhauls per week. It was figure that would only get worse across all three Southern Works as time progressed. Even before anything was started the SR works were collectively short of twenty skilled boiler makers as well as being under pressure to release ninety-one from railway service to the labour exchanges for other (unspecified) work.

Finally, at this time we have the first mention that small supplies of oil – basically a single tank wagon – would be held at other (for the moment unnamed) depots for emergency use.

Two former LMS (LNWR origin) tenders fitted with oil tanks and recorded – we believe – at Eastleigh. Close examination reveals them painted as Nos 5 and 6. Their very presence raises a number of questions, none of which are truly answered. Firstly, apart from a reference after the end of the oil-burning scheme to the 'purchase of two former LMS tenders' (by the SR), we have no mention before this. From the fact they were numbered '5 and 6', does this mean there were others – perhaps not to the same design? The earlier photograph of Lancing (page 14) with the two tenders in the background appears to show a similar design but without oil tanks fitted. Were these in fact the same vehicles later modified as seen? Other images indicate some writing on the inside end, 'Eastleigh' and 'SR Loco' with the letters/initials 'P C J 111 …' Might they even have been used for the storage of heavy oil consumed in the Works? The actual oil tanks fitted would appear to be of the standard type used by the SR (the GWR had their own design but before anyone shouts out that was just the GWR being different again, remember Swindon had adapted some of their engines to burn oil independently and before this 'apparent standard design of tender tank' had been evolved. Later images of what we assume are the same pair of tenders show them dumped on the scrap road at Eastleigh. They remained intact but apparently unused until the early 1960s.

Meanwhile, shortly after we have the minutes of an undated meeting between the SR General Manager, Sir Eustace Missenden, at which just three other persons were present: the Traffic Manager, Mr R.M.T. Richards; the Eastleigh Works Manager, Mr E.A.W. Turbett; and a Mr A.J. Elmes – no mention of the role of Mr Elmes but it may have Brighton Works Manager.

The purpose of the gathering was to confirm the locations for the fixed depot installations on the SR and that there was sufficient room at each site. It was stated the three had been chosen due to their close proximity to a port. There was also a somewhat superfluous note for the time when it was minuted that the GM had expressed a desire for the storage installations to be arranged on modern and well thought-out lines. Perhaps he should have addressed that to the CCE and then took cover for the likely response!

At Eastleigh, converted engines of classes 'N15', 'H15', 'N', 'U', 'D15', 'L11' and 'T9' would be based. At Exmouth Junction, it would be West Country, 'N15' and 'N' classes, and at Fratton, 'L11' and 'T9' types, which in detail meant:

Fratton	13 × T9
	2 × U
	Total 15
Eastleigh	12 × N15
	4 × H15
	10 × D15
	7 × T9
	10 × L11
	15 × N
	Total 58
Exmouth Junction	20 × WC
	3 × U
	4 × N
	Total 37

The Fratton and Eastleigh allocations would include Nos 305 and 740 respectively – already converted. Note also that some slight adjustments have been made to the number of each class it was intended to convert.

Mr Smart commented that while this involved eight different loco types, only five types of tender were involved and if necessary the new equipment could easily be recovered and if necessary transferred to other engines. In reality this was never required to be done or we believe ever considered. At this stage the tender oil capacity was also anticipated to be 3,500 gallons – in reality it would be 1,600.

The minutes reported that the conversions could not be confirmed to one particular class either although, as will be referred to later, we might also wonder if consideration had even been given to all the engines at one particular depot being converted, so rendering a 100 per cent oil operation from that depot, in which case Basingstoke might well have been a better option.

The converted engines were envisaged as working both passenger and freight duties and would be kept active as much as possible. Eastleigh and 'N15'/'H15' conversions were the only ones singled out for some (limited) detail, with the two classes

'N15' No. 748 *Vivien* seemingly hard at work with an up boat train passing Shawford on 31 July 1948. It is probably fair to say the exhaust is 'not quite what is should be'; a brown cloud emerging from the chimney and no doubt at the very least unpleasant to the occupants of the following coaches. This could be the result if there was too much oil or not enough steam to disperse the oil. Of course, there may have been other reasons for the situation, with the simplest being that 'firing' had just recommend and the oil/steam mixture was yet to be synchronised to best advantage. Even so, it is one of the few images located showing a dense exhaust from an oil burner. The range of an oil burner was in the order of 250–300 miles so, allowing for the fact this was a boat train starting from Southampton and considering also the necessary light engine running at the start and end of each journey, a Southampton–Waterloo and return journey could still be accomplished without undue difficulty or the need to refuel (there was nowhere to do this north of Eastleigh anyway!). *W. Gilbert/R.K. Blencowe*

to work Waterloo to Southampton boat trains and Waterloo to Bournemouth passenger services. We also hear the first mention of the actual 'men' (drivers, fireman, shed/refuelling staff) needing to be 'educated' (trained might have been a better word) in the use of the 'fuel-operated engines'. Each engine would carry sufficient fuel to give it a range of 250–300 miles.

For the remainder of 1946, paperwork continues almost on a two steps forward and one back basis, or with work stalled for the simple lack of resources both in human terms and more especially with the supply of necessary equipment for both the locomotive conversions and the depot installations. As has already been stated, clearly not all the records have survived and so statements made cannot be confirmed or indeed refuted.

As examples of this, we are told the railways (general term meaning all three companies – the GWR already had theirs) anticipated having burner drawings to hand by 3 September 1946, then on 16 September 1946 that the actual oil storage tanks for the three depots were to made by the Admiralty but we have no idea for either whether this was later to be the case.

The number of steam-heated tank wagons required had also risen from 775 to 890 – without explanation. These were also to be branded 'Loco Fuel Oil'.

Less than a week later we have a report from one of the regular SR meetings involving the Traffic Manager, CME, CCE, Superintendent of Operations, and Superintendent of Motive Power that were also occurring. No doubt there was a similar arrangement occurring on the other railways. (The M&E Committee were probably also meeting on a regular basis.)

So far as the SR was concerned, it was the Traffic Manager, Mr Richards, who was in the chair and on 9 September he reported both progress as well as recent difficulties.

On the subject of the oil storage tanks, Bulleid reported that he had sent a letter to the Ministry of Fuel and Power to the effect that their bolted storage tanks could not be accepted and that the tanks must be of welded construction. If there was no option, bolted tanks could only be regarded as a temporary measure. If the reader is seemingly drawn to the conclusion that this was Bulleid throwing his weight around as an advocate of welding, take note it was a genuine and valid concern as the oil to be stored (used) had a high sulphur. Add to this the introduction of moisture at the top of the tank as the level of the oil fell, and the resultant combination (sulphur and water) would combine to create sulphuric acid. Hence it was estimated that the life of a bolted tank was only two years.

Basingstoke shed; one of the eight depots on the Southern designated as 'emergency fuelling/top-up depots' under the scheme. No physical work was ever undertaken here, or indeed at the other locations so classified. In this view taken on 7 July 1957, and long after the end of oil burning, 'West Country' No. 34107 *Blandford Forum* stands company with a 350hp diesel shunter and 'H15' No. 30489. *R.C. Riley/The Transport Treasury*

For his part, the CCE, Mr Robertson, produced drawings of the proposed installations at the three SR depots. Eastleigh, with its land available, was not an issue. At Fratton there were two possible locations, with only one mentioned in the minutes as being between the 'new road and the existing hoist road'. Frustratingly, we do not have the plan that was 'discussed' at the meeting!

It was at Exmouth Junction that the real issues prevailed, and here simply for want of space. The consensus was either obtaining more land or temporary storage tanks on raised supports. Again, no plan is available to describe the specific location.

A general discussion also took place on the number of fuelling points to be provided. From an historic perspective this is probably the most fascinating point to come out of this meeting for we learn that the Southern, along with the LMS and LNER, were all in favour of refuelling by means of overhead gantries. Only on the GWR was there ground refuelling and as we know this was already in place, although Swindon were '… understood to have this under further consideration'. Mention is also made of a swivel arm-type arrangement for fuel delivery on the LMS – whether an alternative to a gantry or as part of is not explained.

Mr Richards next states the obvious that it was 'undesirable' to withdraw engines for conversion until the depot installations were complete. With an existing backlog of engines either awaiting or under repair, this would make the prevailing motive power situation even worse. In reply, Mr Bulleid reiterated it would be possible to convert ten engines per week but only on the condition that all the necessary parts were on hand. Surprisingly, we do hear the subject of skilled staff shortages mentioned. Bulleid also referred to his earlier comment on behalf of the M&E Committee to the government that if the engines were required to be running quickly then the whole of the necessary equipment must be sourced by and supplied by them.

What follows next is almost comical, for Bulleid is minuted as stating '… there is already one engine fitted at Lancing for oil-burning – E4 class shunting engine. It was considered this would give an opportunity for some of the staff to get acquainted with the apparatus.' Clearly even the CME was not briefed correctly at times!

At last we also now hear where the emergency fuelling points were to be located, and these were stated as being at:

Nine Elms

Feltham

Basingstoke

Salisbury

Plymouth Friary

Barnstaple Junction

Okehampton

Wadebridge

They would also be at the works at Brighton and Ashford in connection with engines moving to and from each. It was stated ground storage of 4,000 gallons should be available at each, together with an allocated tank car for each depot. No mention is made in the minutes as to whether specific sites at these locations had been selected.

Information also comes in on undated pieces of paper without a recipient or signatory (all most frustrating) but all relevant as pieces of what is becoming an ever more complicated jigsaw. Among the ideas mentioned was that the CME was to convert engines from the selected classes only as they came in for overhaul. This would certainly be an advantage so far as works time was to be concerned but with the disadvantage that it would have taken far longer for the requisite number of engines to be converted. Associated with this was the suggestion that oil-burning equipment should be installed on the next batch of West Country-class engines to be built, again intended to save works time with later conversions. We know neither of these was acted upon, nor for that matter was the much earlier proposal for engines of the 'Q1' class to be equipped for oil burning.

With all this going on and promises having been made in Parliament it was no real surprise when, in 1946, David Gammans MP (Conservative, Hornsey) tabled a question on the subject of 'Oil-Burning Locomotives'.

Mr Gammans asked the Minister of Transport how many engines were to be converted to oil burning; what was the cost of the conversion; and what were the running costs in comparison with coal?

A written reply was received from Mr G.R. Strauss in October 1946: 'Arrangements are in hand for the conversion of 1,217 locomotives to oil burning. I am not yet in a position to give estimates of conversion and running costs. '

It was a nice evasive answer, telling everything but at the same time nothing, although to be fair there was little real factual information to hand at the time. Other more pointed questions would be raised in Parliament later. One, believed to be from 1948, involved the costs and this was neatly sidestepped by the government, who stated that £1.3 million of coal costs had been saved. (What was singularly not mentioned was that the cost of the replacement oil used had certainly far exceeded that figure!)

While we do not know the exact date the Commons question was tabled (Hansard does not assist), we do know a further question was tabled by another MP, Mr Errol, on 19 May 1947. The question was asked of Mr Barnes as to how many locomotives had actually been converted to that date. The response was twenty-three; eight on the GWR, one each on the LMS and LNER and two on the SR – the information provided to Mr Barnes may have been slightly out of date! But what is interesting is when Mr Barnes adds that the process was not being helped by a shortage of steel.

Returning to the railway, we know that another SR meeting was held on 23 September 1946, again with representatives from the same departs present (but not necessarily the exact same individuals). From this we learn that the CMEs had now agreed that they would place their own contracts for required materials and that it was understood the Ministry of Supply would '… give all assistance …' to the requisite contractors in securing the material '… should they (the railway companies) have any difficulty'. This made perfect sense; the railway companies knew exactly what was required and it saved perhaps going through several hands and, we may suspect, a considerable amount of government 'red tape'.

The same meeting also dealt with the issue of the construction of the oil storage tanks and it is immediately clear that Bulleid had not been alone in his refusal to accept bolted tanks other than on a temporary basis. On the SR there would also be what is referred to as a 'temporary' stage, with both Eastleigh and Exmouth Junction each taking one welded tank, and at the same time Eastleigh would have two temporary bolted tanks and Exmouth Junction just one. At Fratton a number of smaller tanks were envisaged, of which all were available and these would be of a welded type. Indeed, as will be gathered, the Fratton installation was deemed to be the most straightforward as time progressed.

The design of the tanks, regardless of type, was such that would be on the same foundations, hence when changeover time occurred it could be accomplished in a straightforward manner. A timescale was also given with the two bolted tanks for Eastleigh, the one bolted tank for Exmouth Junction, and the welded tanks for Fratton all ready for use by 1 January 1947, again with the caveat, '… but the completion date may be later …' We thus begin to understand why the railways were not keen to commit to the conversion of numerous engines only to have these standing out of use until refuelling facilities were available.

Taking the reduced oil capacity into account as well vis-à-vis the intended number of oil-burning engines originally proposed at each of three installations, it was now proposed that a reduction in the converted engines per depot be envisaged. Accordingly, the Eastleigh allocation was reduced from fifty-eight to thirty-eight and Exmouth Junction from thirty-seven to eighteen. Fratton, though, would remain at fifteen as here the requisite tanks would all be available.

The rest of the meeting was devoted to a timescale for engine conversions to take place from 1 November onwards. It appears one difficulty was the supply of the static pumps associated with the storage tanks, about which we will learn much more later.

Never to miss an opportunity, and certainly in the style of Sir Herbert Walker, Mr Richards pointed out that as fire cleaning would not be required on the converted engines, the time so saved could be used more productively and the engine diagrams 'tightened up'. (Years before, Sir Herbert Walker had learned of a derailment of a light engine somewhere on the

'Merchant Navy' No. 21C11 at Salisbury (SR) shed on 26 September 1946. Salisbury was one the depots designated to have a 'topping up' location but no work was ever done here, or at the other locations intended to have this same facility. Without further details we can therefore only speculate how any emergency refuelling would have been achieved considering the heating and pumping requirements designated. It is not believed topping up depots were just to be confined to the Southern. Aside from here at Salisbury, the other intended locations were Nine Elms, Feltham, Basingstoke, Plymouth Friary, Barnstaple Junction, Okehampton and Wadebridge. Presumably emergency supplies would also similarly have been provided at depots on the other railways.
R.C. Riley/Transport Treasury

An example of the atrocious weather conditions endured by the south (and of course elsewhere) in the winter of 1946–47. This is Southampton in January 1947, where snow and ice are having to be cleared from the tram lines before the vehicle may continue. We can only imagine what it must have been like attempting to proceed with the building of the fixed installations at Eastleigh (just 5 miles north) as well as elsewhere at this time. As an aside, we should mention that, whereas on a cold day the cab of a steam engine was invariably a haven of warmth, that was not the case with nearly all the oil burners because on these the firebox door was never opened in service. The exception as to warmth with the fire door closed was No. 21C119, although of course it was not converted to oil until July 1947. Here the design of the Bulleid cab was such as to create a convivial working environment free from draughts.

SR system – it matters not where. Instead of enquiring how and why this had occurred, he instead wanted to know why it was running light in the first place and so not earning revenue!)

Four days after the 23 September meeting, an unnamed individual from the SR wrote to the Ministry of Supply on the subject of the pumps to which they referred. From a response received from the government department we learn that only four pumps from Messrs Hall having a capacity of 40 tons delivery per hour were available, and then not until the end of November. The alternative and it appears preferred supplier of 'Weir' type pumps having a 93 tons per hour capacity stated that it could supply nine pumps by the end of December and the remaining three in January. A representative of the Ministry, Lt Col Stowell, stated they could do nothing to enhance delivery. On that basis the SR confirmed it would be impossible to commence operations with oil fuel at both Eastleigh and Exmouth Junction on 1 January 1947, although the four smaller pumps would be installed at Fratton.

A list was also provided indicating the final number of pumps required per site:

Stage One		
Eastleigh – working at ⅔ capacity		
Fratton – working at full capacity		
Exmouth Junction – working at ½ capacity		
	Pump type: Hall	Pump type: Weir
Eastleigh	6	4
Fratton	4	3
Exmouth Junction	4	3
Totals	14	10
Final Requirements		
Eastleigh	9	6
Fratton	5	3
Exmouth Junction	7	4
Totals	21	12

Meanwhile, we may recall the government stipulating back in the summer of 1946 the need to save coal for the winter period, hence now may be the appropriate time to record a few points relative to the weather scene between October 1946 and March 1947, the conditions of which adversely affected progress on the ground installations:

October 1946: A predominantly dry month, easterly winds.

November 1946: Commenced dry but with moist air and above average temperatures. There was fog at times of a sufficient density to disrupt rail transport. Much rain in the south towards the middle of the month.

December 1946: Further rain at the start of the month but then on 19 December came the start of the really bad weather. Snow and cold temperatures, with 2°F at Farnborough on 20 December. At first it seemed things might improve as a thaw set in on 22 December …

January 1947: From mid-January on there was a penetrating frost with 1°F recorded at Farnborough on 30 January. (It had been even colder at Berkhampstead the previous day, with -13°F reported.) One foot of snow fell on the same day and the sailing of the *Queen Elizabeth* from Southampton was delayed by several hours as boat trains were in turn delayed by frozen pointwork. It is at the SR officers meeting of 20 January 1947 that we find a reference to the weather conditions, for when reporting as to progress at Fratton, the Chief Civil Engineer's representative stated, '… the contract work has been commenced on site, but no definite date could be given for completion, particularly having regard to the present weather conditions'.

February 1947: A slight thaw to start causing localised flooding but by 12 February food and fuel supplies were in crisis with additional restrictions imposed on the use of electricity. As the blizzards continued some families applied for additional coal, wood and paraffin supplies but these were only allocated to those with special needs. The predicted (from the summer of 1946) fuel crisis worsened with businesses either resorting to laying off staff or working if they could by candlelight. A similar reporting position as to progress took place at the meeting of 17 February regarding Fratton, for while excavation work has proceeded with it had not been possible to undertake any concreting.

March 1947: Even more snow fell in early March, with 300 major roads in England blocked and fifteen towns and innumerable villages, hamlets and farms cut off completely. Road and rail passengers were stranded, while telegraph poles simply snapped. Relief came at the end of the month but the thaw brought with it understandable flooding. Of course, the summer of 1947 was then one of the best on record!

And remember, it was through all of this that the Southern Railway and others were expected to continue to proceed with the physical installations, although it was later acknowledged the extreme weather had likely put the whole operation back in the order of six weeks.

Another progress report was issued on 28 September 1946. We may suspect these were as much for the government as anything else. While they likely circulated around certain key individuals, nowhere is it mentioned that 'Mr So and So' will be responsible for the implementation of the scheme. Arguably the man with ultimate responsibility was the General Manager but it also seems that, locally at least, Messrs Bulleid and Richards led the way.

We are informed on the date mentioned that orders for burner boxes and firehole protector plates had been placed with Messrs Clifford Edwards of Hove. Some fourteen sheets of drawings had also been sent to the Ministry of Supply, the North British Locomotive Company and the LMS Inspection Bureau. Exactly what these were for is not detailed and also why they were sent to the LMS – unless, of course, the SR and LMS were sharing information, or maybe the LMS was even acting as a co-ordinator in certain areas?

Locally, the Divisional Engineer had been instructed to clear the depot sites. There is a human angle to this at Eastleigh, where the Estate and Rating Surveyor was directed to contact those who had allotments on the site selected and who were to clear the area of crops forthwith. No mention was made of any alternative site being made available. We may have some sympathy with those affected in this way as only a few years before almost every piece of spare ground had been given over to cultivation to help feed the nation, and with many foods still either on ration or in short supply it was a cruel even if necessary step.

So far as the erection of the storage tanks was concerned, at Eastleigh Messrs Machans had been given the contract, while at Exmouth Junction this was the firm of Mallinson and Murray. At Eastleigh, Machans would be responsible when the permanent tanks were available, while at Exmouth Junction it was Messrs Oxley. Fratton is only referred to with the entry 'unknown'.

Mention is also now made appertaining to practical aspects concerning the tank wagons: the time taken to heat and then pump oil from the tanks to the storage facility, the number of wagons that could be accommodated at each site, and the number of locomotive tenders it would be possible to fill simultaneously as well as the time required for this task. As it transpired, not all these questions would ever be answered. A minor point mentioned was that the SR had located thirty-four unused metal frame windows (it is not stated what these were left over from), but these had now been reserved for use in the boiler houses.

Elsewhere, the file contains a copy of a fortnightly report from Mr Hawksworth at Swindon on how the GWR were progressing, which appeared to be along similar lines to the Southern. No copies of similar reports appertaining to the LMS and LNER were contained in located paperwork.

By 21 October, a note appears to imply the North British Locomotive Company may have been made responsible for the supply of the tender oil tanks. As stated earlier, we also know the government had promised to give the conversions and with it the necessary equipment priority when it came to supply and delivery but there also seems to have been confusion in some quarters as to who would supply what.

Were the railway companies to order directly, quoting the government requirements, or pass their orders to the Ministry of Supply for action at government level. Surviving records are not completely clear on this.

Meanwhile, more information on the specifications for the tank wagons also begins to filter through; these were to be 21ft long, necessary for standard connections to be made at loading/unloading points. On the basis of the number of tank wagons already in use that might then be adapted for their new role, a maximum tolerance factor of 6in was permitted.

We learn more on progress when representatives of the senior officers of the Southern met on 25 November – where any of these meetings were held is not reported – but Waterloo would seem to have been the most likely. For the CCE there was news that the drawings for Fratton were almost complete and that it was anticipated contracts might be signed in seven to ten days. This would be followed 'shortly' by a contract for the mechanical engineering work at the site; pipework, pump, gantry installations. Eastleigh was also mentioned, with progress made on the necessary drawings. Nothing is said appertaining to Exmouth Junction or the 'top-up' sites.

An undated and handwritten note refers to tenders being issued for the supply, delivery and erection of the steelwork at Fratton being sent to seven firms. Three replied they were unable to quote for work, we may suspect for the simple expedient of being unable to guarantee to obtain the necessary steel, although the fact it was 'urgent' government work may have helped. The lowest tender was from S.W. Farmer & Son Ltd for £1,450, which was accepted. As regards the civil engineering and building work at Fratton, we do not have a list of who was invited to quote but we do know that Messrs McAlpine, while invited, did not reply. Of those who did, estimates were stated as being between £8,100 and £9,200; the work being awarded to Messrs William Cowlain & Sons, who tendered the lowest figure of £8,172 1s. A note in the file states, 'The whole of the cost will be borne by the Ministry of Transport.'

The spectre of health and safety also raises its head at this stage, with concern that contractor's men working at Fratton and Eastleigh would need to be given specific access paths to reach their work but would be required to sign indemnities absolving the Southern Railway in the event of accident. Messrs Cowling naturally also requesting that wagons bringing the required materials to the site be shunted as close as possible to the actual work sites.

Of interest too is a report from the Divisional Engineer that at Fratton a new lead had been laid in the trackwork and engine run-round and a temporary siding provided. At Eastleigh the drawings for the layout were in hand. Some idea of the pressure the CCE department was under comes in a pencilled addition to the report. Referring to Exmouth Junction, it states, 'Still plans not started. All available staff engaged on Fratton and Eastleigh.' The predicted difficulties foreseen by Mr Robertson were proving all too accurate.

On 30 November 1946 we return to the subject of the locomotive conversions with the news that the Motive Power Superintendent anticipated he would be able to release forty engines for conversion to oil in the two-month window from 1 November 1946 and 1 January 1947. As the date of the report does not correspond with the start date mentioned, we may ask if this was a misprint or if things or had in fact already started?

For the record, the initial engines types selected for conversion were now also confirmed as:

10 × West Country
2 × N15
4 × H15
2 × D15
10 × N & U
12 × L11/T9

In the event only one main-line engine would be converted in 1946, 'N15' No. 740 – but it did no harm to be a little optimistic! Moving ahead slightly, we could mention that No. 740 was taken into Eastleigh works on 6 November 1946 to emerge on the 14th of the following month as the first of the Southern Railway oil-burning engines; as it transpired the only engine to be converted by the Southern Railway in 1946. So much for having the scheme operational by the end of the year! (We may conveniently ignore No. 515S as it was not counted in the SR total for locos anyway. It is not known if the LMS or LNER similarly converted a 'test' engine. The GWR is deliberately excluded as they already had some main-line engines operating by this time anyway.)

On 17 December 1946, there is mention of a report having been issued appertaining to the supply (or position) on spares, lighting and boilers. Frustratingly, this does not appear to have survived. The mention of lighting, though, is interesting as this was first discussed a couple of weeks earlier on 3 December, when there is reference to electric lighting in the cabs of the engines but nowhere is head/tail lighting referred to. The GWR also had electric lighting in the cabs of their converted engines, so we now ask the question why was it considered necessary? Crew comfort would certainly not have been high on the agenda at that time. Clearly the GWR, as the first operational player, had found this necessary, so likely the Southern were following their lead even if No. 740 had just/or was about to be released into traffic. When this information was shared with the LMS and LNER, both commented they had no such plans.

The Southern had also decided that the Motive power Department would have 'Fuel inspectors' based at Exeter, Woking, Eastleigh, Orpington and Redhill. The first three locations are obvious but we have no explanation as to the final two.

At the end of the year the position as regards the engines converted to burn oil on the four railways was as follows:

SR   1 – again not including No. 515S as this had not been included in the original calculations.

GWR 14

LMS Nil

LNER Nil

Depot wise, on the Southern, Fratton was progressing well with anticipated completion in January 1947, Eastleigh it was hoped by the spring/ summer and Exmouth Junction sometime after. All way beyond the government's required date but then they had made promises on the supply of equipment they must have quickly established were impossible to keep.

In that respect the delays were out of the hands of the railways, as was the weather situation described earlier. As if the add to the tale of woe, there is a late 1946 (exact date unknown) note circulated by the GWR stating that supply issues had forced a suspension of any further conversions. The outlook for 1947 appeared bleak to say the least.

No, we have not gone 'all GWR', but as the reader will gather, it is necessary on occasions to refer back to the other companies, especially the GWR, who had been first on the scene. This drawing again comes from the 1947 R.J. Eaton pamphlet and shows a GWR oil depot (based on an actual location but we are not told where). The salient points, though, of all the installations regardless of location are present, although not shown is the boiler house. The drawing shows the design of tender tank fitted to the engine reasonably accurately and as this is on a smaller GWR tender it could be more rectangular at the top. (Later, when the GWR began fitting oil tanks to their larger tenders, these too were tapered along the sides.) The GWR also used electric lighting in the cab but these were battery rather than generator powered. We get the impression they were also portable rather than fixed lights. Early in 1947 it was agreed that, compared with the other companies, it was on the GWR and SR that experiments would be carried out with electric lighting.

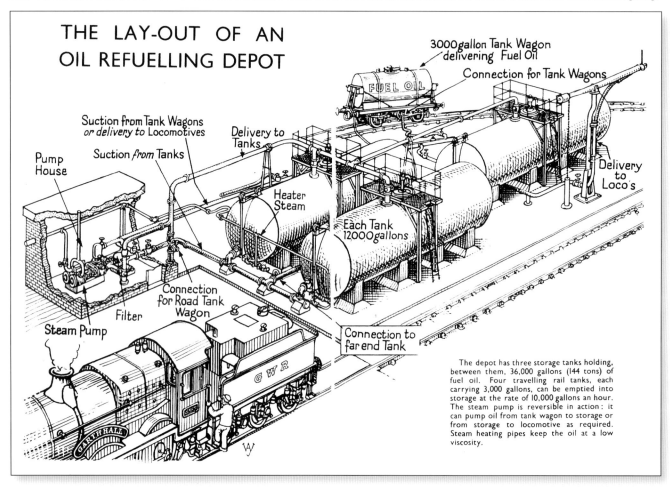

THE LAY-OUT OF AN OIL REFUELLING DEPOT

The depot has three storage tanks holding, between them, 36,000 gallons (144 tons) of fuel oil. Four travelling rail tanks, each carrying 3,000 gallons, can be emptied into storage at the rate of 10,000 gallons an hour. The steam pump is reversible in action: it can pump oil from tank wagon to storage or from storage to locomotive as required. Steam heating pipes keep the oil at a low viscosity.

2
A new start, a new year:
January to September 1947

As mentioned in the previous chapter, discussion and planning had been going on behind the scenes for some time before the August 1946 public announcement on oil firing. An astute fireman might have found the idea appealing – after all, it was a change to working practices and with it the potential for an easier life, while there were also some members of the travelling public clever enough to realise that, by implication, this could well mean trains might become faster quicker and more reliable; as it transpired, a vain hope.

Reported as the first train operated by No. 740 as an oil burner, the 11.30a.m. Waterloo to Bournemouth West recorded at Brookwood in December 1946. Whether this was the normal load cannot be confirmed but on this occasion there were at least eleven vehicles plus a van on the drawbar. With the exhaust a light colour and steam simmering from the safety valves, all would appear well on the engine. On 31 December 1946 it was reported the engine had been withdrawn for attention to the oil supply pipes and firebricks, and possibly at the same time the blastpipe diameter was reduced by ½in.
S.C. Townroe/R.K. Blencowe

However, elsewhere, and not given much in the way of publicity, was disquiet among the miners and National Coal Board. Both had been quick to realise that this change was potentially the first step in reducing demand from what was the largest customer for coal in the UK – the railways. There was certainly no immediate threat for, as we know, locally produced coal was being mainly sent to export markets but longer term, if the use of oil as a fuel was continued and even expanded while at the same time export demand slowed, such a move could potentially result in job losses and pit closures. As it transpired, the limited timespan that eventually occurred with oil firing had neither effect but the issue could well have become a problem for the Labour government then in power.

As to the fuel itself, this was 'Bunker C' oil. This was basically a heavy residue of what remained from crude after the lighter elements had been distilled: propane/butane, petrol, diesel, etc. 'Bunker C' had previously been used primarily in shipping and would indeed continue to be for some decades, while it was also later used in static power stations. Because of its limited usefulness, the import price was also slightly better than that of export coal, hence the advantage perceived by the government.

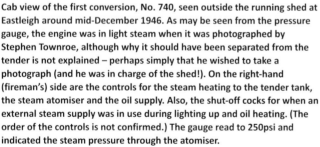

Cab view of the first conversion, No. 740, seen outside the running shed at Eastleigh around mid-December 1946. As may be seen from the pressure gauge, the engine was in light steam when it was photographed by Stephen Townroe, although why it should have been separated from the tender is not explained – perhaps simply that he wished to take a photograph (and he was in charge of the shed!). On the right-hand (fireman's) side are the controls for the steam heating to the tender tank, the steam atomiser and the oil supply. Also, the shut-off cocks for when an external steam supply was in use during lighting up and oil heating. (The order of the controls is not confirmed.) The gauge read to 250psi and indicated the steam pressure through the atomiser.

Another of the Townroe images, this time with No. 740 being moved forward by Inspector Charlie Dear, whose hand is on the regulator. The fitter (?) hanging on to the opposite side is not reported. Note also the group of enginemen, perhaps awaiting static instruction.

One disadvantage of 'Bunker C' was the need to pre-heat it to approximately 140°F (the GWR refer to 180°, so perhaps this higher temperature was found to be more suitable but it should be noted this could also be a simple misprint as 180° is above the flashpoint for the product) before it became suitably viscous. Pre-heating was thus necessary both in order for refuelling and to maintain the oil at a similar temperature on board. Even so, it is interesting to note the tender tanks do not appear to have been externally insulated, unless they were of the 'double-bund' type (a tank within a tank).

The release of No. 740 *Merlin* from Eastleigh in mid-December 1946, while tangible proof the project was advancing, was also only the first step. We should also recall that the depots were not

ready: Fratton was certainly the closest to completion but at this stage the paperwork is also strangely silent as to how and where No. 740 was to be refuelled. Of the engines from the 'King Arthur' class originally scheduled to burn oil, just five would eventually be converted, the remainder being dealt with later in 1947.

No. 740 was fitted with a 'Mexican Trough' ('Weir')-type burner – basically a long trough to which a horizontal fitment was installed across the front of the firebox designed to spray fuel both sideways and forwards (meaning towards the rear of the firebox). The firedoor remained, although in practice this would not be opened during normal working. Instead there was a small spyhole fitted for observation of the fire bed. Other modifications included changes to the grate and a number of additional firebricks being added, likely to the sides and lower half of the firebox. Unfortunately information on the technical aspects specific to the SR conversions is sadly lacking. Similar modifications would have applied to all the converted engines but again we have no detail. It would also be interesting to know by how much the grate area was thus reduced.

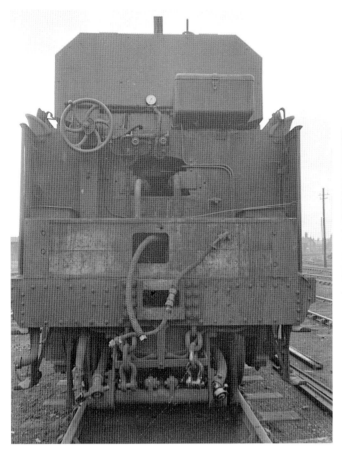

The tender from *Merlin* and with the two extra pipe connections associated with oil burning. The larger of the two is that from the oil delivery, with the second the steam heat supply to the tank from the engine. Notice on the extreme left a pipe outlet by the footstep, which may well be a drain. One interesting point is the position of a thermometer/temperature gauge for the oil. All the tenders would have needed one of these to confirm the temperature of the oil within the tank, and yet on similar views it is missing.

Same tender – same day? It certainly looks like it, but minus the temperature gauge fitment. Perhaps that explained the presence of the fitter and this was therefore a shed and not works fitment. The somewhat substantial tool box will be noted. Compared with a tender full of coal, the height and bulk of the oil tank tender would have restricted visibility during tender-first running. Within the actual tender, the tank was held secure by plates/lugs welded to the tender, so meaning the tank literally was held in place. As such it could not move – but do see the comment about that coupled to No. 749 later! By this method there was no need for bolts or other fixings, which in turn would have created an area prone to corrosion.

For the tender, No. 740 retained its eight-wheel example, into which was fitted a 1,600-gallon oil storage tank (this capacity of tank appears to have been the norm for all the conversions and it weighed in the order of 6–7 tons when full (not dissimilar to the weight of a full load of coal), bolted in the space where coal had previously been carried. We may assume the underside of the tank was shaped to fit the existing coal space as it is not thought there was any change in tender water capacity. The oil tank was of welded construction with at the top two sides tapered along their longitudinal axis to comply with the loading gauge. Two new pipe connections were provided, one for steam to pre-heat the oil necessary for delivery from an external source and the other as an actual delivery pipe from the tender that fed straight to the burner. Filling was achieved by means of the simple expedient of opening a lid on the top of the tank and dropping in a delivery hose. The warmed oil was simply gravity fed from the tender into the firebox, the flow able to be regulated by the fireman. At the same time, he would adjust a steam spray as required.

As first converted, No. 740 was taken around to the nearby running shed, where engine and tender were inspected by staff and Loco Inspector Charlie Dear put in charge of instructing crews (*see* page 32 et. Seq.). Fortunately, S.C. Townroe was also on hand to record some of the accompanying images.

Initial trials involved No. 740 working locally from Eastleigh (details are not given), after which it was sent (light engine?) to the other Southern depots where oil-firing services were intended to operate to and from. These were listed as Fratton, Salisbury, Basingstoke, Bournemouth, Nine Elms, Exmouth Junction, Wadebridge, Plymouth and Barnstaple Junction. This was possibly the only time an oil-burning locomotive visited the actual depots referred to located west of Exeter, although destined not to be the only time an SR oil burner worked west of Exeter. However, it also explains why Basingstoke and Bournemouth are mentioned. (This would be around the time – December 1946–April 1947 – when the 'D1' No. 701S was based at Exmouth Junction (*see* p.69)

No. 740 was deemed reasonable successful in its new guise but soon (possibly as early as the end of December 1946) had its blastpipe reduced in diameter by ½in to improve draughting. (A similar modification is referred to by Andre Chapelon as being a common change necessary with oil-burning locomotives.) We do not know if a similar alteration was made all the other oil burners of the various classes but we do know that the other members of the 'N15' class converted were similarly modified prior to entering service in their new guise.

The intention had been to convert ten members of the 'N15' class, and indeed ten had been earmarked and supposedly laid aside (perhaps 'earmarked' might be a more accurate phrase for there are no reports of a long line of 'N15s' stored pending conversion), although in the event only five were dealt with, the remaining five returning to work in coal-fired mode. As to why specific engines of the class were selected/laid aside/converted, the answer is probably simply that these were the ones due for works visit or necessitating a repair.

(A glance at the *Railway Observer* list of engines arrived for/awaiting works for the period 1946–47 reveals any number of the 'King Arthur' class would fit the criteria as being due for works around this time, and consequently it is not possible to confirm with any degree of certainly which others members of the class might well have been considered.)

	Date converted to oil	Reverted to coal
740 *Merlin*	14 December 1946	20 October 1948
745 *Tintagel*	2 October 1947	18 December 1948
748 *Vivien*	27 September 1947*	20 November 1948
749 *Iseult*	11 October 1947	20 November 1948
752 *Linette*	27 September 1947**	2 October 1948

* Official data/dates may well be when the actual information reached the works offices from the shop floor, as contemporary observation by enthusiast John Bailey refers to No. 748 'fitted and put into service' one day earlier, on 26 September 1948.

** Again, contemporary observation by John Bailey refers to the work on this conversion under way/completed two months earlier on 28 July 1947.

In the event, all five members of the 'N15' class involved were modified at Eastleigh. Nos. 749 and 752, converted in September and October 1947, were also noted as having emerged from Eastleigh fitted with electric headlamps – and presumably tender lamps – powered by a Stone's steam generator; the Southern Railway having decided at some stage between the end of 1946 and this date to provide slightly more than just electric lighting in the cab. The reason for this

No. 749 *Iseult* outside the front of Eastleigh shed 4 September 1948 and, as with No. 745 depicted on the cover, in SR malachite livery and with electric lighting fitted. In the background is one of the 4-4-0s similarly converted. *Mike King collection*

fitment, retrospective on the earlier conversions, may also be related to an incident that occurred at Fratton around September 1947 when spilt fuel oil was ignited from the flame of an oil lamp. Possibly the engine involved was an oil-burning 'T9', but other than being able to suggest an approximate timescale and location, no formal record is known. It is also possible that the Fratton incident occurred after the decision to provide electric lighting had been made. Although in theory a 'sealed' system once in use, oil leakage was, as we shall see later, an issue at times, the most likely location for this being during fuelling or from beneath the burner in the firebox.

Initial works trials with newly repaired/new engines from Eastleigh were usually undertaken by the Works trial crew and involved a short journey to Micheldever, Botley/Fareham or Romsey. It is thought this was unlikely to have taken place with the 'oilers' and instead the conversions were simply shunted around to the running shed to be fuelled and trialled from the adjacent depot.

At this point it is appropriate to bring in the reminiscences of former Eastleigh driver Hugh Abbinnett, then a fireman at the depot and who was specifically interviewed about his experiences with the oil-fired engines some years ago. Fortunately, Hugh had personal experience with No. 740 when first converted: 'Ask any fireman who worked on steam engines

in the late 1940s and he will tell you steam had an inherent drawback; namely, the raising of the necessary boiler pressure entailed so much excessive manual labour. Huge boulders of best Welsh or hard black coal first needed loading on to the tender and had then to be broken up into usable fist-sized nuggets before being fed into a roaring furnace, often at speeds of 80 or even 90mph. [Hugh conveniently fails to mention the general quality of coal more usually available at this time.]

'Of course, also being properly prepared was not easy, and there was always the fireman who had to resort to smashing lumps of coal into suitable size while on the move, which invariably resulted in clouds of dust as well as the wrath of his driver.

'Not surprisingly, any fireman welcomed the idea of being able to raise steam without having to resort to such manual labour. Possibly it was partly in answer to a humble fireman's prayer that in the summer of 1946 work commenced on the building of some large sheds on spare ground at Eastleigh steam depot. Rumour was rife; new fitting shops, test depot, even an oil depot, were suggested. The latter was given credibility with the arrival of some weirdly shaped, matt-black painted tanks that took up residence just north of the loco canteen. At least it made a change to look out and see these instead of a steam engine. All though was pure conjecture until

The same engine, No. 749, but this time waiting at the exit to the shed – the 'M7' in front will have to leave first. Bradley refers to the oil tank fitted into the tender of this particular engine as having the somewhat alarming habit of moving backwards and forwards when running. *Frank Foote, courtesy Mike King*

one evening the Running Foreman, Freddie Springer, crept into the smoke-filled "spare" cabin and in his gentle and apologetic manner murmured to Driver Harris, "There's a few ashes in No. 740 over on the pit. Get your mate to throw the fire out and give the smokebox a good clean, she's over the works on Monday for fitting out for oil burning."

'This was it; oil burning. The wires of the bush telegraph ran hot, exaggeration went over the top; every engine on the Southern was to be fitted to burn oil. No more shovels, no more fires to clean, the job would be a doddle … and so it went on. How quickly the fireman (me) was brought to earth, for on No. 740 those "few ashes" turned out to be a firebox full with one ton of green coal, which some over-indulgent individual had kindly provided. It was an unenviable task to clear out this rank, smoking black mass. Eventually though all was completed and the next day, Saturday, No. 740 was placed outside the shed on No. 14 road ready for the attention of the cleaners. All hands now knew her destiny: the first oil burner [presumably memories were short from 1926!] and No. 740 had to look her best. Up on the boiler, the Chargeman Cleaner, Charlie Ganger, polished her dome while the youngest member of the gang got the roughest job – scraping the wheels and cleaning the rods and motion. The sunshine was reflected in the green gloss of her paintwork, which was embellished with a liberal coating of mineral oil. Even the tender shone, sections of "fielding" caused

where the cleaners had deliberately overlapped the marks of cloths folded neatly into 4in squares.

'Late on the Saturday afternoon No. 740, together with two other engines, was first towed out on to the main line before being propelled back into the works yard, there to await the attention of the fitters and welders on Monday morning.

'It was not long before No. 740 returned again from the works, the tender surmounted by a high black tank giving a definite humpbacked appearance. In the cab there was an additional collection of heavy brass controls. These were located just below the sight feed lubricator on the fireman's side of the cab, almost in front of his small wooden seat. Hardly had she been uncoupled from the "M7" that had brought her from the works than inquisitive viewers were scrambling over her fitments; anything to gain an insight as to what the operation of this oil-fired locomotive might be. Close examination revealed the brass wheels to be for such things as "flashing up" and "priming", with the more knowledgeable conveying this information to others in the cabin. What they didn't know they made up, but it was all well intended because official instruction was often sadly lacking. Who then was going to teach us to operate this new form of oil firing? The answer came with one of the running foremen, Charles Dear, a tall, robust and extremely good-natured man of no small intellect who, it was now recalled, had been absent from his duty as a foreman for

The final convert from the 'King Arthur' class, No. 752 *Linette*, and again at Eastleigh. As with the Bulleid tender just in view on the left, electric lighting is fitted. This was the only member of the converted engines that had already been fitted with a multiple jet blastpipe and larger-diameter chimney by Bulleid. What difference this may have made to the engine's performance as an oil burner is not reported. *W Gilbert/R.K. Blencowe*

some time. It was almost as if the railway, in an act of typical clandestine secrecy, had spirited Charlie away to gain the know-how that he was now to impart to us, the "oiler" firemen.

'"Oiler" was to become the operative slang for all the oil-fired locomotives. In addition to the engines, change at the depot was also spoken about, with a new bypass siding to avoid the tailback of coal-fired engines waiting to take on fuel and, of course, once again rumour was rife. Large gantries were spoken of with six or seven steam-heated oil outlets, while sandboxes would be filled from pressurised sand pipes. Overhead water cranes would also be erected – life would be oh so easy from now on …

'It was not long before we were dragged down to earth again. At Eastleigh, No. 1 shed road was where locomotives were washed out and descaled and where the fitters carried out repairs that could only be tackled with an engine out of steam. Accordingly, around this part of the shed lay the clutter and rubbish associated with such repair work: leather washout pipes, descaling rods, smoke tube rods, plug spanners, all that was necessary to keep an engine at work. One wet morning a large rail-mounted oil tank car with steam-heating valve attached was shunted into the top of No. 1 shed road, blocks placed under the wheels and the handbrake screwed hard on. Again rumour was rife, which nowadays may appear somewhat ill informed: cheap fuel from the Navy, battleships being scrapped, cleanings from the tanks at Fawley, and all at one ½d per gallon. So different from our vision of overhead filling points!

'Shortly after this, a Brighton tank engine was placed by the tank and used to heat and pump the fuel, although again not before the know-alls had their say. According to them, this engine was also to be used as a permanent standby in case of a fire on one of the "oilers", although the vision of this diminutive engine wheezing its way to where it was needed was, to say the least, in the best tradition of Heath Robinson. [Hugh does not mention it but the Brighton tank had previously been fitted up as a fire-fighting engine, hence it is easy to see how such a story might start. There was certainly never any intention or indeed possibility of continuing the use of the "D1" in a dual role as both a fire-fighting engine and an oil pump; besides, water on an oil-based fire would have no effect other than to spread the flames.]

'Meanwhile, Charlie Dear had not been idle and with the tank engine secured to the tank wagon by a multitude of pipes and connectors, the first sets of men for training on oil firing were selected and instructed to sign on duty at 8.00a.m. Monday morning. The crews soon found there was a distinct disadvantage to the use of oil fuel – the smell. Upon arriving for duty, No. 740 was seen attached by pipes to the pump and storage tank while the warmed fluid slowly seeped into the tender. The smell hung around in the air, heavy and all pervading, similar to that of creosote on a summer evening. The oil was also a filthy fuel, far worse than coal, and a brush past one of the delivery pipes would leave a smear on one's light blue overalls that belied all attempts to remove it. A partial solution was found with paraffin, though later an even better cure existed and that was to use the liquid contents of the fire extinguishers fitted on each "oiler". Consequently, fire extinguishers fitted on the "oilers" and then in every other

location were quickly drained into bottles to be used as a cleaning agent. Meanwhile, Mr Dear, having satisfied himself that there was sufficient fuel in the tender, instructed the first crew to "flash her up", and with a turn on the atomiser valve it was possible to observe a black spray start flowing into the firebox. A well-soaked paraffin rag held in the priming tongs was then set alight and the whole burning mass pushed through the firebox door.

'Now came the sound every "oiler" man was to get to know and love – "whoof" – and a quick glance in the firebox revealed it immediately to be a raging inferno as the spray from the atomiser became a burning fountain. Another glance, this time at the chimney, revealed that for the present at least too much oil was being presented into the firebox, as from the chimney rolls of heavy oily black smoke were evident before settling down on to the previously beautifully clean engine. This heavy black smoke was destined to be a long-lasting problem on the "oilers"; it drifted over stations, staff, passengers and even allotment holders, all of whom complained bitterly. The latter group were particularly vociferous and many an angry remark was heard from a man whose cabbages were now covered in black or by someone who had lost his prize chrysanthemums. Eventually the effect of reducing the oil flow at the atomiser worked and the black smoke gave way to a light grey, which finally cleared to heat haze. By this time the water in the boiler gauge glass was starting to jump around slightly, a sure sign of steam being raised and with it the pressure gauge moved slowly off its stop. With a few pounds of steam raised, it was possible to use the blower, which allowed a greater draught to be created and consequent rapid production of steam. No. 740 was now independent of the tank engine and was duly uncoupled, placed in forward gear and the brakes released. [This implies the D1' was also providing a steam supply for the atomiser to work. Townroe refers in similar form later but we have no information as to where this steam supply was coupled on to No. 740 from outside.] Each man was then instructed individually by Mr Dear, which included moving the engine up and down the shed yard. Included in this instruction was the word "economy", always a regular component of railway vocabulary. Charlie Dear, in his pep talk, added phrases like "flash up here" and "close down there", for it was quickly found that once No. 740 was hot she could regain full steam pressure at the turn of a wheel, instantaneous steam as never experienced before by students of the shovel.

'On the road it was found there were other disadvantages as well as the smell. One of these was that the atomiser nozzles would choke and thus combustion was ruined, while the additional rows of firebricks laid in the firebox had a habit of collapsing. In addition, "flame outs" were not uncommon where, as the name implies, the flame went out but oil was still being delivered. Within a previously hot firebox, the result was the copious production of black smoke.

'Management quickly found a way to ease the lot of the fireman even further and this came with the provision of a delightful steam-driven electric generator, which was almost like a new toy to the crews. No more cleaning oil lamps, gauge lamps and primitive flare lamps, the latter being no more than a few cotton strands sitting in a bath of oil, with light being produced from a flame at the end of the spout. Instead, the simple expedient of the turning of a valve would set the generator humming and with it the various controls would be illuminated by a strong white light where previously one had groped in perpetual twilight. How primitive our colleagues on a conventional coal-fired engine now seemed. On the road the engines were almost universally loved, mainly due to the reduction in manual labour. Each crew could also tell its own story about the engines, like the one with the "T9" that, having only 160psi boiler pressure, would leak so badly when the flame was extinguished that pressure was lost in a matter of minutes. Then there was the incident at Eastleigh shed, caused only because of a lack of experience. On this occasion an "oiler" was slowly making its way down to the water columns,

S.C. Townroe had a journey on one of the oil burners (we suspect it may be No. 740) and recorded this set of images to indicate the exhaust colour. It is believed they were taken between Eastleigh and Fareham. Possibly because he was on board, no excess smoke is detected!

although its progress was blocked by a line of coal burners on their way to the coal hopper. Accordingly, the crew of the "oiler" jumped off, leaving their steed. A little later the queue moved off again, although this time there was no one to move the next engine and it was left to a young cleaner to assist.

'Such a move was, of course, against all the rules but it was already a time-honoured tradition that firemen and even cleaners would assist the shed drivers in moving engines when necessary. In the cab the cleaner soon found the engine was extremely low in steam. A little knowledge though can be dangerous and with the words "flash her up" ringing in his ears, he opened the atomiser. This was a reasonable move as with the firebricks still red hot it was to be expected that she would roar into life. For some reason, though, this failed to occur, while the young lad did not attempt to ignite the liquid that was now running down the inside of the firebox. Eventually it began to drip and form a puddle on the ground under the engine where, as "luck" would have it, some hot ashes and clinker remained. Ignition did then occur but not quite as intended for the whole of the outside of the engine was immediately enveloped in flames. With fire leaping all around him, the young man cowered in the corner of the cab quite expecting to be incinerated at any moment. But help was at hand for the noise of the explosion had already alerted some drivers and firemen nearby, who rushed to the scene. One, Driver Spicer, had the foresight to jump on to the engine behind and charge at the blazing machine, so carrying both engines away from the blazing fuel, after which the flames

At the same time we have this pair of cab views, with the fireman intent on observing the pressure at the atomiser. George Blakey, in his recollections of the oil-burning engines at Fratton. mentions that with the fireman now concentrating much of the time on the oil/steam mixture within the firebox, it was not uncommon for him to forget to keep an eye on the actual water level in the boiler. He adds, 'I do not know of anyone actually coming to grief ... I believe there were some near misses.'

quickly subsided and it was possible to mount the footplate and turn off the oil spray. Incidents such as this were generally few and far between, partly because the lifetime of the oil burners was so short. No. 740, for example, took another trip to the works to emerge once again as a coal-fired machine ready for another fireman to "throw out her ashes". Most of the other classes were never reconverted and lay in the back road at Eastleigh awaiting scrapping. Meanwhile, the fireman laboured on with paraffin lamps and wicks and those lovely steam generators just corroded away. Fond memories, then, of the "oilers", yes there were some. Of the driver watching his crew mate gently swinging his legs on his seat and passing the snide comment that the fireman's lot was now easier than his own. But the smell: it stayed in your nose and throat and on your clothes for weeks. Perhaps the coal-fired engine was harder work but it was certainly a lot healthier.'

We should now return to the more formal agenda but for which the surviving paperwork has a number of blanks relating to dates of meetings and reports. We know, for example, that on the Southern senior officers meetings were being held at least every month and this would explain the first located report being for 3 February 1947, although after this there is no record of progress until June. (A separate 'internal SR' meeting involving we do not know who on 31 March noted that parts were now to hand to convert one of each of the SR types to burn oil.)

As at 3 February we can at least say that 'T9' No. 305 had been converted, emerging from Eastleigh on 18 January (contradicted elsewhere in the official paperwork when the date of 23 January is spoken of) with the intention it would straight away go to Fratton for training and familiarisation. At this stage both Nos 740 and 305 were being referred to in the official paperwork as 'experimental conversions'. Instruction on the 'oilers' was not limited to loco crews either as, although not mentioned in the paperwork, fitting staff, steam raisers and boiler makers especially would have needed knowledge of the changes made. The February paperwork also gives the first indication of the number of men now trained on the oil burners (probably meaning just No. 740), which at Eastleigh was twelve drivers and thirteen firemen, and at Fratton twenty-two in each grade. Why the greater number at Fratton – well, it is likely to have been due to the fact that even at this stage is was apparent that this would be the depot to be completed first and would then have a greater number of engines operating. The February report gave no further news on the supply of tanks for the emergency refuelling points. Had all 110 intended conversions taken place and on the basis of two crews per loco, then a minimum of 220 loco men would have needed to have become familiar with oil fuel operation. This would have meant a major effort by the railway for in March 1947 there was still the belief that all 110 intended conversions would be ready by the end of the year.

It would be tempting now to refer to the first sign of dark clouds appearing on the scene, and nothing to do with those that might emerge as a result of incomplete combustion or extreme weather conditions. Instead it comes in a memorandum from Bullied to Sir James Milne dated 14 March 1947 and clearly responding to earlier correspondence from Paddington.

Bulleid states as follows, 'In reply to your letter of 7 March, the difficulties are not difficulties in the CME department.

'At the meeting of the M&E Committee on the afternoon of the 11 inst., it was agreed to report as follows – As from the 1 June it will be possible to fit 100 engines per week, provided that the ground installations are completed, that tank wagons and oil are available and the complete sets of locomotive fittings be delivered at the said rate commencing on 1 May 1947. We have in fact a positive assurance that supplies of oil will be available as required.'

Then a somewhat surprising sentence, 'We cannot even get small items of materials to enable some of the installations on the GWR practically ready to be completed and it is obvious to me that unless the Cabinet issue very clear and positive directions that this conversion is to have the highest priority and that supplies of materials are to be carried out, all the locomotives will not be available for next winter.'

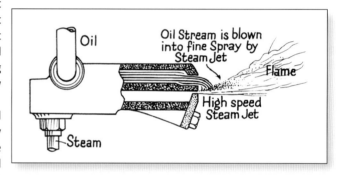

Sketch of the firebox burner. Although again taken from the R.J. Eaton booklet, it is believed to be a good representation of the type used in most of the converted SR engines (excluding No. 21C136 later). The point to note here is that ignition would take place from the point where the oil and steam jet first combined. Care had also to be taken to ensure the steam atomiser was not set to too high a pressure or there was a risk of the flame literally being blown out. One other point not mentioned by Eaton is that it is believed the oil-burning engines also carried a bucket of sand on the footplate. This was because, unlike the char and ask created by burning coal that, as it passed through the boiler tubes, would in effect scour these, with oil burning the opposite took place and an oily film would built up on the inside of tubes that was detrimental to steam production. Consequently, at intervals the firebox door (or was it an inspection hole?) was opened – naturally too with the burner at a low level – and a handful of sand thrown in. This would be caught in the blast and so forced through the tubes, having the same effect as cinders/ash. However, compared with coal – where this scouring was a continuous process – with oil (sand) it was only at intervals and we might only imagine the 'clag' that would have emerged from the chimney on such occasions.

So why was Bulleid talking to Sir James about work on the GWR? Surely this would have been more likely to have been the GWR's own CME Hawksworth? The answer seems to be that Bulleid, as Chairman of the M&E committee, was thus responsible.

More importantly the issue of equipment, supplies and oil come to the fore. It would be a position on all three that would continue to be raised in the months ahead.

Meanwhile, on 2 April 1947 a letter was received at Waterloo from the National Union of Railwaymen appertaining to

The converted 'T9' No. 305, which was despatched to Fratton for familiarisation training. It is very likely No. 740 had similarly visited the depot but No. 305 was intended to be based there. Until June 1947 (excluding 515S), Nos 740 and 305 were the only two oil-burning engines working. In this undated view, No. 305 is seen piloting 'B4X' No. 2071 southbound near Nursling with a through Cardiff to Portsmouth working. The two SR engines would have taken over the train at Salisbury. *Jeremy Staines collection*

concerns over health and safety on the oil-burning engines. Strangely it fails to give any detail as to what these health and safety issues might have been and instead refers to the NUR's preferred method of oil firing, which was of the 'Hardy' type. This system was similar to that which had been used in places in the UK years before and differed from the present in that a small bed of coal was still provided but with oil then sprayed directly on to the burning coals. Either the NUR were misinformed as to what was now in operation or there was a deeper meaning in their letter that was not explained at the time. Either way nothing further was heard.

The most useful report comes from the meeting of 16 June 1947 at which we learn of actual progress with the ground installations, etc. Why the long gap between meetings? Well, the temptation is to say there was nothing to report or the paperwork is simply missing, but alternatives may be worth considering although it must be stressed this is pure supposition on the part of the present writer and is based purely on ideas that have come to mind from research into the subject. The first is that the weather in the early part of the year played its part in delaying physical ground work. The weather reports have already been given and need not be elaborated upon again, but if the ground was impossible to work then there would be little to report, although it is surprising there is

no formal mention of weather-related delays in the paperwork. Perhaps this was the chicken and egg situation again; no installations – no point in further locomotive conversions.

Perhaps more relevant was that the urgency had started to evaporate. The country had managed to find its way through the winter fuel crisis and with summer seeing a reduced demand for coal, the scheme was no longer at or near the top in the list of government and consequently railway priorities. As stated, there is nothing to support this conjecture but it is interesting to report that nowhere in the regular reports is there mention of urgency being displayed by the government as had certainly been the case previously. We may also ask if the securing of items needed was still on a 'priority' basis? It was almost as if the grand scheme was now recognised as being impossible to deliver in such a short space of time.

We learn then on 16 June 1947 that, as regards Fratton, there had been no deliveries of oil pipes, steam pipes, oil valves or steam valves since 19 May, although three storage tanks had arrived.

Meanwhile, 'frantic demand' requests had been sent by the SR to the Ministry of Supply on 10 May for the remainder of the required Fratton material. This only elicited the response that *most* of the material would be supplied by mid-June. (The italics are those of the present writer.)

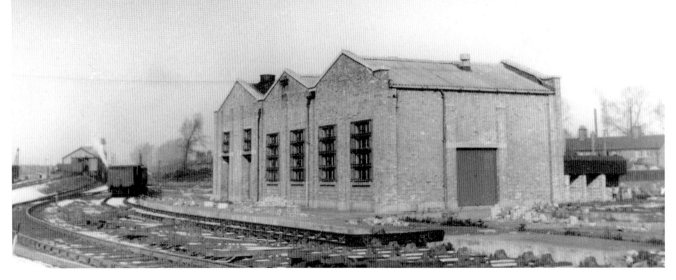

We turn now to the installations, of which illustrations and plans are extremely limited. This single image by S.C. Townroe shows the buildings erected at Eastleigh comprising the boiler house and pump room. The same style was used at Fratton. Townroe records this as having been taken in May 1952 and so after the oil storage tanks had been removed (the latter together with those at Fratton were subsequently bought by the Chandlers Ford-based plant hire company Messrs Selwoods), possibly some other items may also have been taken away by this time. Notice, too, what is almost certainly a tender oil tank behind the building. The photograph is also useful as we have a 'placing' for the installation using the coaling stage and rear of the houses in Campbell Road as reference points. Although, as referred to in the text, there was some discussion about subsequently using the buildings for diesel shunter maintenance, it is not believed this was ever done and they were subsequently demolished. *Tony Molyneaux*

Taken from the very useful R.A. Cooke track plans, the area occupied by the Eastleigh oil depot – but minus the buildings – is identified.

Pump house equipment, Eastleigh and likely similar at all three installations.

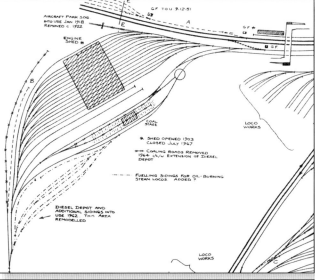

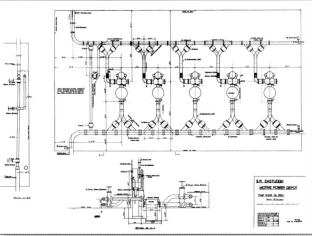

A brief glimpse at part of the exterior structure of the Eastleigh installations. (The 'USA' tank is irrelevant to the story in hand.) *Roger Thornton*

It also becomes apparent that despite an obvious list of 'priority headings', 'frantic demand' being just one (purely for interest sake what might the others have been; 'urgent', 'priority' etc, etc …?) there was still little actual progress in securing material, without which it was just not possible to complete the ground installations. The example was that in February the MoS had promised to have all material available for Fratton by 30 April, for Eastleigh by 31 May, and for Exmouth Junction by 30 June. Direct communication with the actual suppliers did not appear to have any real effect either, with example replies such as: from the supplier of pipes, '… in a few days'; valves, '… the middle and end of June'; and filters, '… will do all that is possible'. No mention is made of equipment for the emergency refuelling points.

From a reporting perspective this same paperwork provides us with a useful resume of the physical position of the work at each site to date:

Fratton
Divisional Engineer's Work:
Permanent Way installed – 65%
Drainage – 70% *(57%)*

Contractor's Work:
Concrete Mat – 30% *(5%)*
Brickwork for Buildings – 75% *(45%)*
Total Civil Engineering Work – 54% completed *(42%)*

Two views now of engines around the vicinity of the oil depot at Eastleigh. Depicted are 'L11' No. 411 and from the same class No. 157. Both would appear to be out of use and stored, so we may therefore date these as being between October 1949 and the spring of 1951. (The chalked writing on the framing of No. 157 is unfortunately illegible.) Note the position of the electric generator on both and associated wiring/piping. No. 411 especially looks abandoned; minus its smokebox door handles and with the electric lights minus their bullseyes. (Were these the same type of brass-cased electric lights fitted to the Bulleid Pacifics?) It is, however, the backgrounds that afford the most interest; behind No. 411 we have another glimpse of the boiler/pump house – I am not sure though about the brick walls that appear to be of the same sort of build – footings for a flat-bottom oil tank perhaps? But now look at the background to No. 157; we have what are clearly pipes (salvaged or just not used) *and* a gantry behind. Could this be an incomplete gantry that was intended for refuelling? We know the Southern were not keen on ground filling and preferred the idea of a gantry/column arrangement. If so, this is the only (part) image located. We just need to move the engine a bit to confirm! No. 157 was also the engine seen sometimes shunting the goods yard at Poole. *Mike Morant collection and Peter Swift collection*

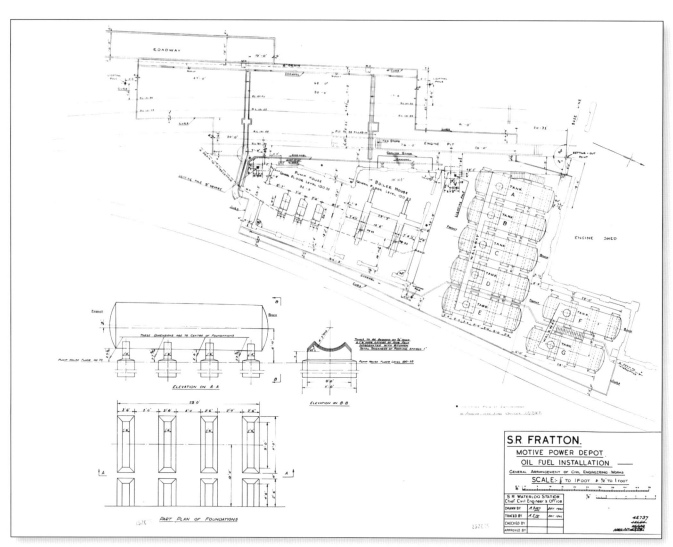

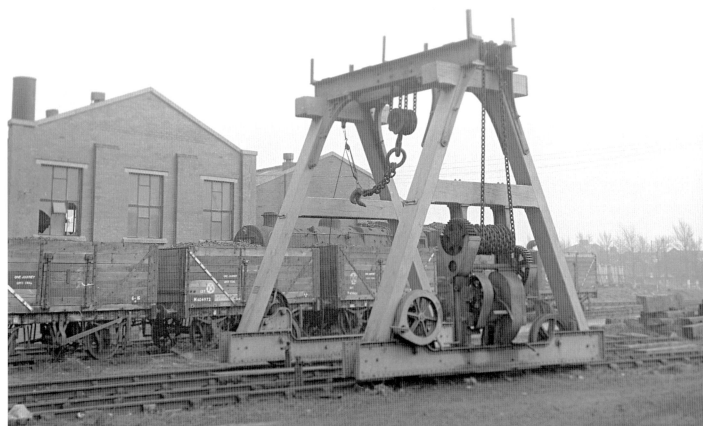

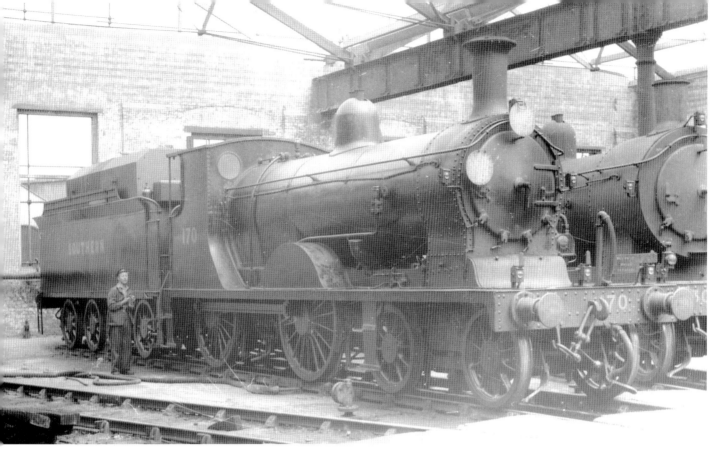

Above: We now move inside the roundhouse at Fratton, where 'L11' No. 170 was recorded in 1948 and no doubt prior to the cessation of oil burning. The engine may well be being prepared and it is worth noticing the oil stains on part of the bunker tank, while to the left of the tool box on the tender may be glimpsed a fire extinguisher. (Is the pipe on the ground related in any way to raising steam?) George Blakey refers to these 'asthmatic' engines being given a new lease of life with oil. The headcode is not one that appears applicable to any known working of the oil burners. He also mentions an occurrence that could have had far more serious repercussions. This was when the night fire lighter (steam raiser) was involved in preparing the oil burners for their next day's duty and after lighting all the engines he inadvertently fell asleep. Unfortunately one of the engines (a 'T9') raised pressure a bit faster than anticipated and the pressure in the atomiser blew out the flame in the firebox. The oil, though, was still flowing, producing a heavier than air gas that seeped out of the firebox along with by now dripping oil. A passing fireman noticed what was happening and alerted the fire lighter, who immediately set to relighting the fire in the firebox but which now contained a mixture of highly flammable gas ... The resultant explosion ignited the gas and oil within the engine and the pit, causing much damage to the motion of the 'T9'.

Right: 'T9' No. 305 out of use at Fratton in 1948, so likely post-October of that year. The point of interest, though, is not the engine (once more in the way of the background!) but instead we have what appears to be an oil bowser in the background. Note especially the thickness of the pipe with its insulation leading to gantry level. Other intended conversions were 4-4-0s Nos, 165, 168, 407, 410, 413 and 414. *R.K. Blencowe collection*

Eastleigh

Divisional Engineer's Work:
Filling excavated area with hardcore – 30% *(10%)*
Permanent Way installed – 64% *(62%)*

Contractor's Work:
Excavation for footings – 30%
Storage tank foundations – 30%

Opposite top: We move now to Fratton and the only one of the three depots to be completed and come into operation. The ground plan shows the two boilers within the building, as well as what could be two refuelling gantries crossing the pair of running lines. Seven storage tanks are also shown, each resting on ½in thick by 1½in wide layers of hair felt impregnated with layers of bitumen, the total thickness of the packaging approximately 1in. The storage tanks themselves were 9ft in diameter × 32ft long. A steam 'ring-main' was provided into the eastern side of the shed feeding the respective shed roads; this was to allow an oil burner to be lit up within the shed. (The conditions within the shed when this was done could not have been pleasant.) The construction company Messrs Cowlings were involved in the buildings both here and at Eastleigh, and is believed they actually commenced work right in the middle of the big freeze around 20 January 1947. Just one week before this, on 13 January, the supply of parts needed for the ground installations had been noted as a problem. *British Railways*

Bottom: Although taken for the purpose of showing the wheel hoist at Fratton, we also have a view of part of the boiler house. Similarity in design with that at Eastleigh is immediately apparent, although no doubt with detail differences to suit the different locations. *Alec Swain/The Transport Treasury*

Exmouth Junction
Divisional Engineer's Work:
Site cleared.

Civil Engineering Contracts:
The contract for Exmouth Junction has been let to Messrs Cowling & Co.

But we should also doubt whether the percentage figures quoted are strictly accurate, for alongside some a lower percentage figure was shown in pencil – these are the figures shown in brackets alongside. None then perhaps quite as advanced as officialdom might have wished. (It is implied but not confirmed that some preparatory work on the foundations at one or more of the three locations may have been carried out by Southern Railway men prior to the formal contracts being issued.)

So let us pause for a moment to consider. June 1947 was basically the first anniversary of the start of the scheme; a scheme that had been intended (by government) to be operational by 1 January 1947. From a standing start the Southern had really done rather well, although as we continue to see, it was still hampered by a lack of both manpower and equipment resources.

Despite these setbacks, Waterloo were certainly still attempting to proceed, the General Manager's permission sought to place a contract for the erection of pipework and for Eastleigh with the Brightside Foundary and Engineering Co. at an estimated £9,200, the same company having indicted they would be able to work at all three depots simultaneously.

The positive news was that three tanks had been delivered and placed on their foundations at Fratton. The firm of Messrs Machans Ltd was unpacking and cleaning two bolted tanks at Eastleigh, while the material for one welded tank had arrived at the same depot.

The representative from the CME's department also reported that an 'L11' and a 'West Country' were presently in the shops at Eastleigh for conversion, while Ashford were converting a member of the 'N' class. (These were respectively Nos 437, 21C119 and 1831.)

By now at Eastleigh fifty-two drivers and the same number of firemen had been trained, and at Fratton the figures were respectively forty-five and forty-six.

A meeting is referred as having taken place on 28 July 1947 but the records for this appear not to have survived. Consequently we move forward to the next date of 26 August 1947, where details of delivered items were given but which may be best summarised again by the respective depot progress reports – this time the percentage figures given were seemingly not questioned.

Fratton
Divisional Engineer's Work:
Permanent Way installed – 65%
Drainage – 98%

Civil Engineering Contract:

Concrete Mats – 90%
Brickwork for buildings – complete
Roof cladding – 80%

Pipe and Plant Contracts:
Pumps erected with connecting oil pipes and valves.
Boilers in position
Tanks in position. Work on tanks held up by non-delivery of valves.
Pipework 40% complete.

Eastleigh
Divisional Engineer's Work:
Rolled Hardcore Filling – 65%
Permanent Way – 66%
Drainage – 35%

Civil Engineer's Contract:
Brickwork for buildings – 25%
Foundations for pumps and boilers – 45%
Storage tank foundations – 65%

Pipework and Plant Contacts:
Boilers placed on foundations in No. 1 boiler house.
The contract for the erection of the pipework and plant has been placed with the Brightside Foundry and Engineering Co. Ltd. Messrs Machans Ltd, the erectors for the bolted tanks, have been advised that the erection of No. 2 tank can proceed at once. There is not sufficient materials at the site to enable pipe erection to commence.

Exmouth Junction
Divisional Engineer's Work:
Permanent Way – 85%
Drainage – 10%

Civil Engineering Contract:
Storage tank foundations – 25%
General Civil Engineering work 7%

Pipework and Plant Contracts:
The General Manager's permission has been given to place the contract for pipe erection with the Brightside Foundry and Engineering Co. and the Secretary has been asked to obtain a firm tender.

Again now we must pause to attempt to deal with two fundamental issues; the installed boilers and the method of firing these, and about which, yet again, there appears to be no information. So on that basis let us for the sake of completeness attempt to draw some conclusions. The boilers would have been those from Southern Railway stock – ex loco-type – but we may assume not necessarily all identical. Secondly, as to the method of firing these, common sense would dictate that as this was an oil-burning installation the boilers would indeed run on oil. That therefore is the premise, and we have no information to the contrary.

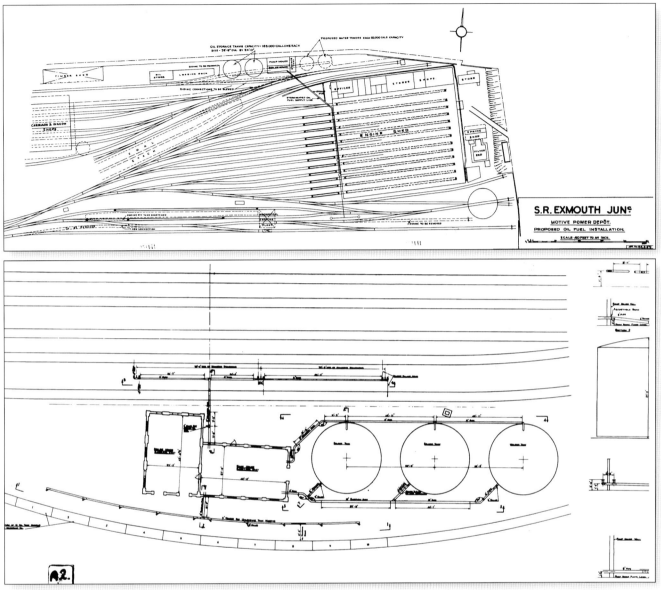

Top: **And so to Exmouth Junction, where we have a ground plan for the proposed installation. No date other than to say 'SR days'.** *British Railways*

Above: **Exmouth Junction was also the one location where space was most at a premium. Even so, the engineers managed to squeeze everything in but this time with three vertically mounted tanks. Alongside the edge, the numbered and curved track indicated now many tanks cars might be unloaded simultaneously.** *British Railways*

The solitary view of the Exmouth junction installation that has been located but with the principal subject, of course, the locomotive (No. 35024 undergoing some maintenance that necessitated removal of part of the casing and totally unrelated to oil burning). In the background above the engine may be seen the same style of buildings with one of the oil tanks in good view. After the cessation of oil burning – although we doubt the tanks were ever even fitted – it is believed they found a temporary new use as additional water storage at the depot, where supplies were prone to become critical, especially at the height of a summer Saturday.
RCTS CRA 0156

As with Eastleigh and Fratton, so an engine was sent to Exmouth Junction and the outlying depots for 'visiting'. This was 'N' class No. 1625, converted at Ashford in the autumn of 1947 but fitted with electric lighting as seen here in February 1948. As described in the text, during this time one of the 'D1' pumping engines was also based here with tender top-ups accomplished from an adjacent stabled oil tank car. We are not informed now many crews from Exmouth Junction may have been trained in oil burning. The West of England headcode is also somewhat appropriate. *Lens of Sutton*

Away from the conjecture to the reality, and the same meeting reported that Fratton would be in use (officially) by the end of October and possibly even the end of September. Concurrent with this date was the plan to have all fifteen engines allocated for Fratton as oil burners to be ready for that date, while fifty-nine drivers and fifty-nine firemen from the depot had also been trained, which, to quote the report, meant it: '… will enable us to bring the whole of the 15 engines into use.'* (At the same time, the Eastleigh figure for trained men was seventy and seventy.)

In an ideal world it would be wonderful to be able to report the date that the first revenue-earning trains hauled by an 'oiler' operated. Indeed, might it even have been that the familiarisation training for crews could have involved regular booker workings; considering the number of men this would seem likely. But in the same vein, even if used just for familiarisation training, the engines involved in this would have needed to have been refuelled and from the foregoing we know the fixed installations were simply not operational yet. As to how the tenders were then refilled, we can only assume this was using one of the converted 'D1' tank

engines to which Hugh Abbinnett referred. Regrettably, yet again we have no dates as to when this might have commenced but from a practical perspective it would have had to have been right at the start of 1947 in order that No. 740 might be refuelled.

We now move away to the trials and tribulations of the SR's Chief Civil Engineer, Mr V.A.M. Robertson, on whose shoulders much of the responsibility for planning and implementation rested. Mr Robertson produced a detailed report on 22 September 1947 sent to the General Manager, perhaps at his own (clearly frustrated) behest or maybe even to deflect criticism that was being levelled at his department. We also learn immediately that some other (unlocated) correspondence from Mr Marsden had proceeded this. It is worth recording Mr Robertson's reply in full:

'Mr Marsden's memorandum of 17 inst., which sets out a copy of a letter from the MofT signed by E.W. Godfrey, is in my view an admission by the Ministry of Fuel and Power of not only a gross neglect of duty by the Country but one of entire lack of foresight and planning.

* It is interesting to speculate that Fratton was also the home depot for a number of 'Terrier' tanks working the Hayling Island branch. Was there then discussion about converting these to oil as they were in effect based at an oil depot, especially with the experience of 515S? Indeed, was this why No. 515S had been converted in the first place? Possibly the lack of real success with such a small engine and the fact that the 'Terrier' working the branch required refuelling at least once during their daily work may have been the governing factor.

'As you will know, I have for nearly 15 months been engaged on the design and construction of oil fuel depots at Fratton, Eastleigh and Exmouth Junction. The difficulties in getting on with these works have been really enormous, but we have gradually got over them and today we are 92% complete at Fratton, and shall be ready to open next month. Progress at Eastleigh is 43% and at Exmouth Junction (the last to be started) 20%.

'In order to arrive at this position I had to put one third of my design staff in my New Works Office, together with a Senior Assistant, on to the work, to say nothing of entirely transferring my Tracing Staff for months on end to the large number of plans required. My two Divisional Engineers concerned, who are supervising the constructions of the Depots, have continually pressed on with the work, a considerable portion of which at Fratton and Eastleigh having been done with our own departmental staff to the exclusion of, and in my view, far more important work on the Railway. My Quantity Surveying staff has been severely pressed in getting out the necessary contract documents in connection with the buildings and equipment.

'All my people engaged on this work have been impressed with the urgent necessity of completing the work as quickly as possible and a great deal of overtime has been worked. I would add that we have all worked as a team against very great odds and I feel that we have done well. We have of course kept in touch with the Traffic Manager and Chief Mechanical Engineer through the periodic meetings held by the Traffic Manager and the Chief Mechanical Engineer has arranged his engine conversion programme to suit the programmed opening date of the Depots.

'May I leave you to judge the feeling that will exists when it is generally known that there is now no hurry over the programme?

'Why the Ministry of Fuel and Power could not have ensured months ago that their distributive capacity was adequate to deal with all demands I find difficult to understand.

'I would respectively disagree with any suggestion that we should consider cancelling work on the ground installations as suggested by the Deputy Chairman (?) of the REC in the memorandum dated 18 September 1947. I recommend that so far as my work is concerned we should complete the depots and ground installations. Work is proceeding, contracts are let, the matter is organised and it would, in my view, be unwise to stop now and start again when things may be more difficult and certainly more costly than they are today.

'I attach some details of the work involved, staff engaged and hours employed, together with a list of some of the more important authorised works which have been delayed owing to the drain on technical staff caused by the preparation of the drawings in connection with the oil fuelling schemes. There are in addition a number of important works under consideration in respect of which the preparation of drawings has been delayed.'

Resume of work:

1. The work in connection with the design and construction of the oil fuel depots at Fratton, Eastleigh and Exmouth Junction has taken nearly 15 months.

2. The present position is as follows:
Fratton – 92% complete
Eastleigh – 43% complete
Exmouth Junction – 20% complete

3. To achieve this it has been necessary for one third of the design staff in the new works office together with a senior assistant to be put on to the work specially, in addition to which the entire tracing staff had also to be put on to the work.

The two Divisional Engineers concerned who are supervising the construction of the depots have had to transfer a considerable portion of their staff to the work, to the exclusion of other work.

The quantity surveying staff have also been severely pressed in getting out the necessary contract drawings in connection with the buildings and equipment.

4. The Chief Mechanical Engineer has had to arrange his engine conversion programme to suit the programmed opening dates of the depots.

5. The total number of drawings which have had to be prepared is 140, made up as follows:

    Fratton – 44
    Eastleigh – 62
    Exmouth Junction – 34

The total number of technical staff employed fully or part time on the work is 27. Time- ordinary 2,192 days; overtime 1,679 hours.

Supervisory PW bridge and building staff engaged on work, man/hours (approximately) 103,000.

6. No fewer than 14 major authorised works have had to be postponed owing to the drain on technical staff.'

Mr Robertson then produced his list of delayed works, titled 'List of Authorised Works delayed owing to drain on technical staff caused by the preparation of drawings etc for Oil Fuelling Schemes'.

Blackfriars Goods – Restoration of roof over ground floor of Hopton Street warehouse and repairs to 'A' Bond.

Bricklayers' Arms – 'G' shed paper warehouse – adaptation for continental traffic.

Canterbury East – Remodelling of goods yard.

Elephant and Castle – Restoration of local line platforms and reconstruction of booking hall.

Fratton – Motive power depot – reconstruction of war damage.

Wartime bomb damage at Malden, as was suffered on 18 August 1940. This was as example of the repair/improvement work delayed due to the Chief Civil Engineer being compelled to concentrate his resources on the oil burning installations. *RCHS Spence collection*

Havant – Rearrangement of station.

Malden – Restoration of war damage and improvements at station.

Orpington – Accommodation for control staff above ground.

Redhill – Accommodation for control staff above ground.

Southampton Central – Accommodation for control staff above ground.

Victoria – 130 Wilton Road, office accommodation for Continental Department, etc.

Wimbledon – Rebuilding of 'A' signal box.

Redbridge – New foundry building.

Clapham Junction – Reinstatement of roof, No. 5 platform.'

So, a year since the public pronouncements and fifteen months since the Southern had started work, and it must be said with some gusto as well, the whole programme was now open for question. In that respect one can feel for Mr Robertson and his team. Of the three railway companies, the LMS, LNER and SR, who had started the whole exercise from scratch it was the Southern, albeit the smallest, who had achieved the most. Exactly whether this report from the MoT was made public at the time is not certain, we think not, but what we may be certain of is that the other two big companies must have been delighted. In practical terms, they had progressed only a small distance, while not to put too fine a point on it, the GWR had almost been hung out to dry over the whole episode, having started off with what was to them a good idea, the government getting involved and then being told to back-pedal. What we do not know is if this curtailment was due to currency issues, the practical aspects of obtaining the necessary hardware from the factories and suppliers, or a simple realisation that, having managed to cope through the winter of 1946–47, it could not be any worse in the coming winter. The trouble with the human race is that we have short memories; the very issues that had caused the proposed conversions to oil firing could very well reappear later.

The reader could also be excused for thinking that could well be the end of the saga so far as the Southern and therefore the subject of this work. But instead there is more: more locomotive conversions, more depot information and information on the trains worked and experiences in operation. Time wise we are not even up to the halfway point yet!

3
Keep b*******g on!

The above quote is supposedly attributable to the country's wartime leader, Winston Churchill. Out of office since the July 1945 general election, had he been involved in the oil fuel situation we might well imagine him saying something along similar lines.

However, clearly with the steam (deliberate pun) taken out of the whole situation it is also understandable that the amount of paper records similarly decrease.

It appears also from odd notes that the Petroleum Board were having some difficulty in allocating sufficient rail tanks to the venture. Remember, these were not just required for

'L11' No. 437 in Platform 1 at Southampton Central. The headcode is not explained but it well be a Portsmouth-bound service. This was the first of the class to be converted to oil in July 1947 and judging by its clean condition it could well have been recorded soon after this. Electric lighting was added later in January 1948. It is ironic in some ways that this addition (and cost) was made to so many engines even though it was known at the time oil burning was likely to be curtailed. Repairs are also taking place to the station in consequence of war damage. *Jeremy Staines collection*

occasional use either, each would be working a circuit, likely a block train working, operating between the port/refinery and the respective depot. They would thus be in continual use and, unlike an open wagon that could well carry a return load, the tank cars were definitely single-purpose only. One suggestion genuinely intended to assist the matter came from a Mr North of the Outdoor Machinery Section at Eastleigh and was sent to the General Manager's Office at Waterloo on 29 October 1947:

'I understand the coal/oil conversion scheme is particularly held up through shortage of wagons for fuel oil. I would suggest that tenders from scrap locomotives could be used for this purpose. It would be a simple job to insert a steam heating coil and fit adaptor couplings for the flexible hose. If necessary a few of the fuel oil tanks made for the engines could be superimposed on the tenders to increase this capacity, this would permit the conversion of a larger number of engines to oil burning and make more use of the installations at Eastleigh and Exmouth Junction.'

'T9' No. 305 detaching itself from its train at Salisbury and carrying the headcode for (Fratton) duty by 371. (Unfortunately a working we do not have details for.) The view was taken on 11 September 1948 and consequently the engine had less than three weeks' work left before it would be stored. GWR oil burner No. 5083 *Bath Abbey* is also known to have visited Salisbury working from Westbury. *Mike King collection*

A not-too-good image of 'T9' No. 314, this time at Southampton central Platform 3; Portsmouth and Southsea to Salisbury working. One serious point not covered in any of the official paperwork is the effect of oil firing in a tunnel. So far as the routes operated by the oil-burning engines, there were a number of these to pass through, dependent, of course, upon the service: Popham, Micheldever × 2, Wallers Ash, Southampton, Salisbury, and if working to Exeter, Buckhorn and Honiton. This was in addition to some of the longer 'bridges', St Cross for example. It would certainly not have been pleasant for crew or passengers if at that moment a change had been made to burner/ atomiser settings. Indeed, later on the Western Region when the Gas Turbine No. 18000 was running on the same type of fuel, 'Bunker C', the smell of the burnt oil was reputed to have had a mild laxative effect. *Jeremy Staines collection*

As a comparison to the previous view, here is how No. 314 appeared when first converted in September 1947 and when it lost time later in the same month while working the 9.45a.m. from Winchester Cheesehill to Southampton. Cleanliness was not always possible in the post-war years and what cleaners were available would invariably be tasked with engines booked for the prestige turns. No. 314 would probably never be as clean again as she was when photographed. *Jeremy Staines collection*

On the surface a sensible and well thought out suggestion, although whether Mr North was aware of the corrosive properties of the oil is another matter. Even so, his suggestion was passed on and generated a response dated 5 November, unfortunately with an indecipherable signature:

'The present partial hold up in the conversion of engines to burn fuel oil is due to distribution difficulties domestic to the Petroleum Board, one factor in which is a temporary shortage of rail tank cars. I understand that the Petroleum Board have acquired a large number of ex RAF petrol tank cars, but these cannot be used for fuel oil until they have been modified by fitting steam heating coils, standard oil fuel outlets etc. It is anticipated that the difficulties will be overcome in April of next year.

'The responsibility for the delivery of fuel oil at out depots is that of the Petroleum Board.

'The scheme for conversion to oil burning covers industry in general as well as locomotives,* and in fact the amount of oil being taken by the railways is a very small proportion of that required throughout the Country. At one time it was suggested that rail tank cars marked 'Loco. fuel only' should be allocated to the railway companies, but this was objected to by the Petroleum Board, who insisted that the fuel should be delivered in tank cars belonging to their own Pool. The

* Mention of conversions other than railway is interesting but out of scope in this work. However, moving forward, perhaps the railways were just another victim when 'time' was finally called upon the scheme.

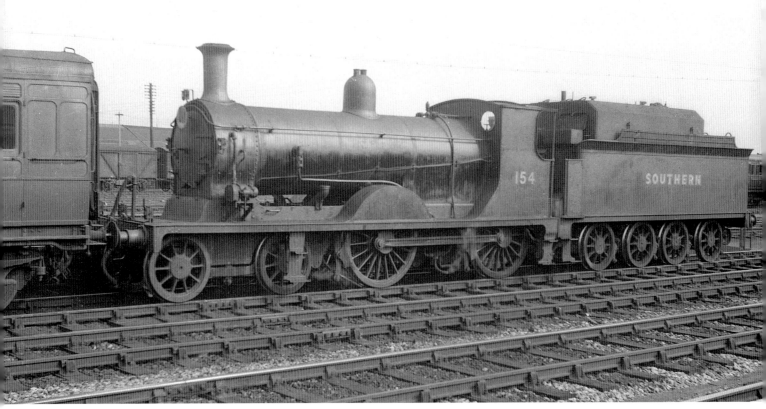

A somewhat work-stained 'L11' No. 154 at Eastleigh Platform 3 and seemingly due to depart shortly for Southampton tender first. Again the visibility issues associated with the tender-first running are apparent. Notice also the lid of the tool box on the tender is open. Taking an average of the conversion costs for each engine but across all four railways, a later memorandum from the early 1950s put the costs of each conversion as having been £435, although no doubt the figures at the start were greater. Even allowing for the value of the pound at the time, it would still seem to be a reasonable figure. Whether this included the cost of the tender tank (unlikely) is not reported. *Arthur Taylor*

reason given by the Board was that at their depots such as Fawley and Avonmouth, they deal with many hundreds of tanks cars during the course of the day and that it would seriously disrupt their internal organisation if they were called upon to segregate special tank cars for the Railways. They desire to accept, say, twenty empties simultaneously, despatch another twenty loaded cars from their Pool, and for this reason alone I am quite sure that the Petroleum Board would not entertain non-standard vehicles constructed from old loco tenders. In any case the number of scrap tenders available would be very small and would be entirely insufficient to meet our requirements.'

Next follows am interesting summary relative to the situation on all four railways so far as the locomotive conversions were concerned (right):

While probably circulated to all four railways, a pencil note referred specifically to the SR conversions and makes for interesting reading. Referring to the fifteen converted engines at/due to be based at Fratton, it asks, 'What happens to the 14 converted not shedded at Fratton in the interim?' It continues, '31 actually converted. It is proposed to store three, leaving 17 at Fratton and 14 at Eastleigh to be utilised as available oil fuel facilities are available, at Fratton and by rail tank.'

Date Converted	SR	GWR	LMS	LNER	Total
October **1945**		1			1
November		2			2
December		1			1
January **1946**		1			1
February		1			1
May		4			4
June		1			1
October		1			1
December	1	2			3
January **1947**	1	2		1	4
March		1			1
April		3			3
May		6			8
June		2	5		7
July	2	4			5
August	5	4			8
September	14	1	4		19
October	6		8		14
	29	37	17	1	84

Months with no conversions taking place are deliberately omitted.

Views of the three members of the converted 'N' and 'U' classes on trains appear to be conspicuous by their absence. Here though we have the solitary converted 'U', No. 1797, with what is likely a through train terminating at Portsmouth, and seen between Portcreek Junction and Fratton. *Denis Callender*

This is most interesting and also most useful. A discrepancy in converted engines first, and which is likely explained that work was still going ahead on others at the time the information for the table was gathered. As all four companies were involved, it is likely it had taken a little time to assemble the information, by the M&E committee perhaps?

Then we have mention that three of the conversions were to be stored. Which ones and where? Certainly in the latter case at one of the two depots – we may conveniently ignore Exmouth Junction in this respect. It would be tempting at this stage to try and put loco numbers/classes to the months mentioned, but we have done this later as per the tables on p.72.

Perhaps most interesting of all is the mention of fuelling, 'available' at Fratton, 'and by rail tank' at Eastleigh. This means both depots were now operating oilers, although again no firm date is available as to when this had first commenced.

We now temporarily move away from the meeting rooms and depots of the Southern Railway and back to Parliament, where for 17 November 1947 Hansard records an exchange between several MPs, including Commander Allan Noble MP (Conservative, Chelsea), Mr Joseph Sparks MP (Acton), Mr Frederick Erroll MP, Mr Quintin Hogg and Mr James Callaghan (Labour, Cardiff South [and later Prime Minister]) then serving as Parliamentary Secretary to the Minister of Transport.

Commander Noble asked the Minister of Transport how many locomotives would be converted to oil burning between then and the end of the year, and in the next six months respectively.

Mr Sparks asked the Minister of Transport what steps were being taken to speed up the conversion of locomotives on the four main-line railways from coal burning to oil, in view of the fact that the necessary storage installation equipment would be completed by the end of February 1948.

Mr Callaghan: Ninety locomotives have so far been converted, and three more will be dealt with by the end of the year. The actual rate of conversion must depend on supplies of oil.

Commander Noble: Will the Parliamentary Secretary give an assurance that this conversion is still being proceeded with?

Mr Callaghan: Yes, Sir. The railways have done a lot of the work on the ground, but we not want the conversions to outrun the supplies of oil.

Mr Errol: As the Minister of Fuel and Power has said there will be sufficient fuel oil available for all the conversions why is there all this delay?

Mr Callaghan: Well, I am not the Minister of Fuel and Power.

Mr Quintin Hogg: The hon. Member soon will be.

Clearly matters on the ground were moving faster than government were prepared to admit to Parliament for, despite the exchange and assurances recorded, we know from at least 17 September the urgency in the whole operation had diminished.

Before moving on the actual train workings and locomotive experiences, two final minuted items documents need reporting. The first is a useful breakdown of the costs the Southern Railway would be submitting ('invoicing' was not the word used in the contemporary paperwork) to the Ministry of Transport. The necessity for these came in a request from the REC and was sent to the Chief Mechanical Engineers and Chief Civil Engineers of each of the four railway companies, with copies also passed to the respective General Managers.

The three depots were referred to individually, thus:

Fratton

General Civil Engineering Contract	£8,820
Divisional Manager's work	£6,616
Pipe erection contract	5,934
Lighting and Water Dept.	£500
Signals & Telegraph Dept.	£500
Outdoor Machinery Dept.	£250
Chief Mechanical Engineer's Dept.	£400
Value of old boilers supplied	£2,000
Overheads	£3,128
	£28,148

Eastleigh

General Civil Engineering Contract	£25,000
Divisional Manager's work	£13,176
Pipe erection contract	£9,158
Lighting and Water Dept.	£500
Signals & Telegraph Dept.	£500
Outdoor Machinery Dept.	£250
Chief Mechanical Engineer's Dept.	£400
Value of old boilers supplied	£4,000
Overheads	£6,373
	£59,357

Exmouth Junction

General Civil Engineering Contract	£21,000
Divisional Manager's work	£6,284
Pipe erection contract	£11,031
Lighting and Water Dept.	£500
Signals & Telegraph Dept.	£500
Outdoor Machinery Dept.	£250
Chief Mechanical Engineer's Dept.	£400
Value of old boilers supplied	£3,000
Overheads	£5,371
	£48,336

Other than the above amounts, there is no separate breakdown of costs on the locomotive conversions.

Finally for 1947, we have a copy of what is marked as a confidential report from the Railway Executive Mechanical Committee on the progress of the venture as at 27 December 1947:

In submitting the following Progress Report, the Liaison Officers, desire to call attention, on this occasion, to the following points which emerged at a meeting they attended on 30/12/1947, under the Chairmanship of General Wrisberg (M/Supply) and at which Sir Mount and other representatives of M/Transport were also present.

1. A decision as to the policy to be pursued in future regarding the continuation of erection work at storage depots is entirely dependent upon a statement from the Ministry of Fuel and Power regarding the quantity, and rate of delivery, of fuel oil which will definitely be made available to the Railways. Sir Alan Mount undertook to seek this information from the Ministry of Fuel and Power.

2. The contracts placed by the M/Supply with a large number of firms contain no 'break' clause and, in the opinion of that Ministry the saving in respect of outstanding items of equipment would be so small that

This time we are at Bournemouth West sometime between January and October 1948 with 'T9' No. 118 awaiting departure – again from the headcode the destination is likely Portsmouth. Note also the tender tool box is on the opposite side, although it appears from photographs some of the eight-wheel tenders also had tool boxes on either side. Official paperwork refers to the fact that 131 tender tanks (invariably of different designs) had been received as early as 4 January 1947. Although not stated, it is likely all came from the North British Locomotive Company. We may realistically assume as well that these were distributed across the four railways. By 15 March 1947 this total had increased to 373 but, of course, not all would end up being used. Their physical size, built to conform to the loading gauge, would also mean they could be transported in one piece to the various railway workshops carrying out the conversions. *Mike Morant*

At first glance this image might appear to be related to the earlier similar view taken from a higher angle (the latter courtesy of a pedestrian footbridge that crosses the line at this point), however closed examination reveals that despite it being the same engine, 'L11' No. 437 and similar stock, the coupling rods are actually in a different position. We also have an 'interested' observer on the central island platform. Mention has already been made of the corrosive properties of the oil used and the fact that the oil tank fitted to the tender of No. 749 had a tendency to move while running. No other specific tender defects or comments are mentioned, while a study of the tanks themselves would also indicate they were of all welded construction.
Jeremy Staines

these contracts should be completed with the possible exception of the second stage welded tanks. This would mean that the Railways would need to provide suitable storage facilities for this equipment.

3. Contracts have been let and the material will be forthcoming for the erection of the second stage storage tanks during 1948, and if these contracts are cancelled it would mean that the original 1,229 engines to be converted would have to be reduced to approximately 600 owing to the consequent reduction of the storage capacity which has been based on 14 days supply considered essential by the Petroleum Board.

4. According to M/Supply records 95% of the ground installation equipment and 99% of the locomotive equipment has either been delivered to the Railways or was ready for despatch, waiting minor details and/ or packing cases. Pending definite information regarding supplies of oil – see item (1) above – it is the OPINION of the Liaison Officers that:

(a) If no more oil than that at present being used for the 93 engines already converted is forthcoming, then it may

be possible, by re-distribution of the locomotives, to reduce further expenditure to the minimum consistent with operating requirements.

(b) If additional quantities of oil, over and above that new being used (5,000 tons per month) but less than the full requirements of 70,000 tons per month, are forthcoming, then it will be necessary to review the whole position in the light of this information having regard to the operating problems involved.

(c) In the event of total, or partial, cessation of work on ground installations, then Railways will be faced with the problems of (i) providing satisfactory storage facilities for the redundant equipment pending its disposal, (ii) restoration of silos, and (iii) cancellation of contracts, placed by the Railways, in which there are no 'break' clauses.

The report continued with statistical data relating to the status of the depots on the all four railways and in general terms.

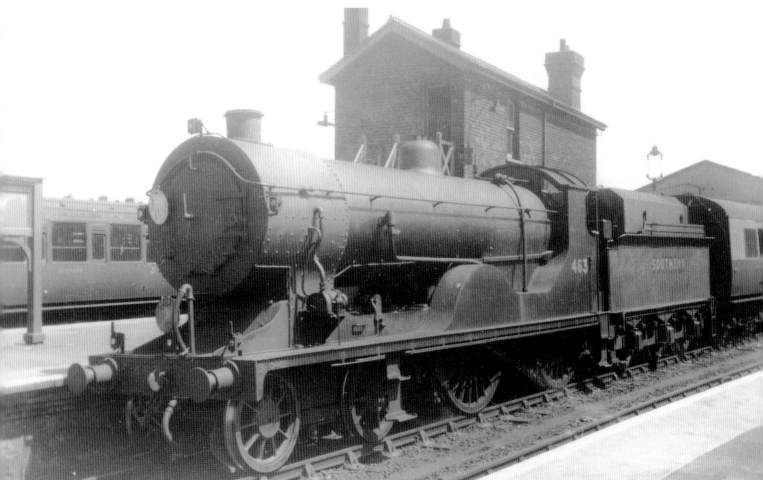

Above: **Another new location, this time Bournemouth Central, and 'L11' No. 437 seen in the art of shunting its train. While both passenger and static images of the engines in their converted state have appeared, we have yet to uncover any view of an oil burner working freight. We do know, of course, there were freight and shunting turns. The picture was taken between July 1947 and January 1948, the latter time when electric lighting was added.** *R.K. Blencowe*

Right: **Rear three-quarter image of 'T9' No. 713 at Fratton awaiting to proceed to Portsmouth. One delightful story concerns the crew of one of the engines working a train between Portsmouth and Southampton. For no doubt intentional reasons, the oil supply was turned off en route, allowing the engine to continue with no fire. There was nothing wrong with that at all as the normal action of turning on the oil allied to the atomiser would create a flammable atmosphere that would spontaneously combust from the residue heat in the firebox. For whatever reason, this seems not to have occurred on this occasion and recourse was made to an out of course stop at Northam Junction, where the signalman was prevailed upon for 'a light' as both crew members were non-smokers and therefore carried no matches. Singed eyebrows could also result when attempting to light or relight the oil vapour with the fire door open. (Did any of the class visit the Harbour station?)** *Bluebell Railway Archives*

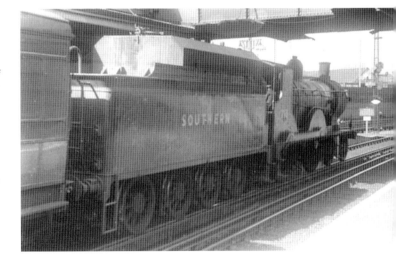

Opposite top: **No. 740 *Merlin* entering Southampton Central on what may well be a service from Salisbury terminating here. (The 'King Arthur' class were prohibited from running on the Netley line to Fareham. An amusing aside into the oil burning of the period comes in a memorandum from the Deputy General Manager at Waterloo dated 13 March 1947, which stated, 'The General Manager would be glad if you would give consideration to the possibility of extending the oil burning engine arrangements so as to provide for an oil-fired locomotive to haul the "Bournemouth Belle" and "Devon Belle" trains with a view to avoiding criticism that coal is being consumed to run luxury trains.' Presumably this was addressed to the Traffic Manager, although the recipient's name is not given. At the time No. 740 was the only large engine so far converted but it is not thought the request was ever acted upon. As stated, the idea was to deflect criticism at a time when other services were being delayed or may have even been curtailed due to shortages and poor-quality imported coal.**

Opposite bottom: **The 'D15' No. 463, also at Salisbury, on 14 May 1948 and about to detach itself from what is a through train to the Western Region. There were no real bad reports concerning the performance of any of the oil-burning engines once any initial teething troubles had been resolved and as such it is slightly unfair to label one conversion better than the next. No. 463, though, seems to have especially received praise and, as mentioned in the text, was often to be seen on Waterloo workings. It would appear then to perhaps have been the only converted 4-4-0 to have workings trains in and out of the terminus. From the sample working diagrams in the text it would appear that at least one oil-burning 4-4-0 would have 'over-nighted' at Salisbury between turns.** *B. Knowlman/R.K. Blencowe collection*

An excellent view of 'L11' No. 148 at Andover Junction in final condition. The GWR loco shed is in the background (dealing with trains that came south on the MSWJ route). From the look of the boiler casing, an amount of priming has also taken place. Electric lighting is in place but we do not know how often this might have been used – or if oil headlamps still resorted to. The fitting of electric light on the engines might almost seem to be an admission that management were aware of the flammable risks associated with oil fumes. However, these were difficult to control on a steam engine. What never appears to have been fitted were any obvious signs cautioning about the specific fire risk. This is perhaps surprising but may well have been covered in the training given to crews. Certainly at this period few of the staff would have had any experience with any petroleum products, excepting perhaps paraffin.
Rev. A.V. Mace/The Transport Treasury

No. 749 again, the one with the 'moving tender tank', on a down boat train passing Vauxhall. It is not known if any tender swaps look place within the classes, while in addition, other than the breakdowns referred to, no accidents or derailments are known of. The original intention had been for oil-fired engines to be identified with a white-painted star in the centre of the smokebox. This would indicate to signalmen that the train did not have to be sidelined into a loop or refuge siding for the fire to be cleaned, as was often the case with coal-fired engines running on the poor-quality coal of the period.
S.C. Nash/Stephenson Locomotive Society

4
In service: successes and failures

We move now to the actual operation of the converted engines in service.

No special oil consumption trials or tests were carried out on the SR – but we may wonder about 21C136/34026 later, although folklore has it unofficial tests between an 'N15' and a 'Caste' were mooted but never took place. This comes from contemporary discussion with staff at Eastleigh during the time oil fuel was being used and reported in the notebooks of the

'T9' as BR No. 30286. Very few of the 4-4-0s converted to burn oil were renumbered in the post-1948 '30000' series, and of those that were none ever carried a BR smokebox number plate. As No. 286, the engine was converted to burn oil in September 1947 and on the 18th of the month was recoded at Romsey in charge of the 7.57a.m. service to Salisbury. On 28 October it was recorded as receiving (unspecified) repairs, presumably at Eastleigh. The BR identification was added in May 1948, with the number also painted on the front buffer beam.
J.H. Aston

late John Bailey. It is possible the Southern Railway/Region Test Section from Brighton were involved but at the present time we have no confirmation. Where we know Brighton was involved was in the drawing office, which had been responsible to most if not all of the locomotive conversion drawings. The NRM Southern Railway/Region drawing register includes countless examples of drawings applicable to all the locomotives classes scheduled to be converted including the 'H15' class, but curiously there is not one drawing for the 'Terrier' conversion.

Official paperwork also reports as follows: 'Performance of oil-burning locos very satisfactory superior to coal burning. Because 31 locos have been operating without the corresponding ground installations as planned no improvement in operation or utilisation has accrued.

'The following casualties have occurred directly due to oil burning:'

Date	Train	Time lost	Engine No.	Cause
30-9-47	9.45a.m. Winchester Cheesehill to Eastleigh	50 minutes	314	Oil control valve seized.
22-10-47	8.10a.m. Bristol to Portsmouth	37 minutes	115	Brick arch defective.
7-1-48	4.57p.m. Fareham to Southampton	37 minutes	713	Faulty oil indicator.
31-1-48	6.57a.m. Southampton to Waterloo	2 minutes	752	Intermediate oil heating pipe broken.
15-4-48	4.35p.m. Portsmouth to Salisbury	11 minutes	1797	Defective plate front of firebox.
11-7-48	10.00a.m. Plymouth to Portsmouth	22 minutes	114	Back air vent taper pin sheared off.

Just five failures in ten months would seem to be impressive, but it must be appreciated we have no benchmark against which to gauge the number/frequency or failures compared with a coal-fired engine, nor if any other defects occurred on the engines that were not oil related. For interest sake, we are also not told where on the line these failures occurred nor what consequential delays to other traffic may have resulted.

We also have a most interesting record of the number of miles run by each converted engine for the two-week period ended 15 May 1948.

Loco Number	Class	Mileage worked	Number of weekdays in traffic
113	T9	1,733	10
114	T9	274	4
115	T9	75	2
118	T9	846	10
121	T9	–	Nil
148	L11	818	8
154	L11	625	10
155	L11	–	Nil
157	L11	1,168	9
170	L11	709	11
172	L11	627	10
280	T9	746	8
286	T9	–	In shops
303	T9	1,051	9
305	T9	–	Nil
314	T9	1,968	10
411	L11	626	5
437	L11	136	6
463	D15	2,266	10
713	T9	–	Nil
722	T9	238	6
731	T9	1,001	9
740	N15	–	Nil
745	N15	985	10
748	N15	1,073	9
749	N15	721	7
752	N15	1,026	8
1625	N	1,475	10
1797	U	1,559	10
1831	N	1,281	11
34019	WC	–	Nil
		23,027 miles	202 days

So why the nil returns and why also count only the weekdays (remember at that time Saturday was also counted as a weekday)? We have no answer to either.

Statistically then, and excluding the zero-mileage engines, twenty-four out of thirty-one oil-burning locomotives were active in the period, covering a total of 23,027 miles. Averaged out, each working engine was achieving just under 96 miles per day, hardly economic and hardly efficient. But again statistics can be misleading, for if we take the best and worst performers, respectively 'D15' No. 463 and 'T9' No. 115 respectively, we find the figures for each day to be 226.6 and 37.5 miles, this taking into account the actual number of days worked.

We also have two other documents relating to the oil-burning engines, the first a list of trains worked by the engines and the second an (almost) complete list of duties worked.

Trains worked by Oil Fuel Engines
Passenger unless otherwise stated

1.46a.m.	Eastleigh	Portsmouth
4.52a.m. (News)	Eastleigh	Portsmouth Harbour
5.23a.m.	Fareham	Portsmouth
6.00a.m.	Portsmouth	Southampton Terminus
6.00a.m.	Southampton	Waterloo
6.23a.m.	Portsmouth	Southampton Terminus
6.36a.m.	Winchester	Southampton Terminus
6.55a.m.	Portsmouth	Southampton Central
6.38a.m.	Eastleigh	Fawley
7.29a.m.	Portsmouth	Salisbury
7.54a.m.	Eastleigh	Andover
8.02a.m.	Southampton Town	Portsmouth
8.06a.m.	Fawley	Southampton Terminus
8.13a.m.	Southampton Central	Romsey
8.20a.m.	Eastleigh	Basingstoke
9.03a.m.	Eastleigh	Portsmouth
9.03a.m.	Portsmouth	Winchester
9.20a.m.	Andover	Eastleigh
9.30a.m.	Southampton Terminus	Winchester Cheesehill
10.34a.m.	Salisbury	Portsmouth & Southsea
10.45a.m.	Winchester	Southampton
11.05a.m. (Vans)	Fratton	Eastleigh

From the same class, this is No. 114 seen in store at Fratton on 3 March 1951 – notice the sacking tied around the chimney. This alone indicates 'storage' rather than being dumped, although as is mentioned in the text, none of the 4-4-0s are reported as having worked after October 1948. In its converted form, No. 114 had been based at Fratton, indeed we do not know if depot allocations changed during their brief life – it could only have been to Eastleigh anyway. The RCTS 'Locomotive Allocations' listing for early summer 1949 reveals no fewer than fourteen engines in store at Fratton as of 21 May. Of these, eleven were former oil-burners.
Bluebell Railway Archives

11.26a.m.	Portsmouth	Andover
11.57a.m. (Vans)	Southampton	Eastleigh
12.28p.m.	Eastleigh	Romsey
12.45p.m.	Southampton Terminus	Portsmouth
12.56p.m.	Portsmouth	Romsey
1.28p.m.	Romsey	Portsmouth
1.15p.m.	Eastleigh	Alston
2.05p.m.	Romsey	Eastleigh
2.03p.m.	Portsmouth	Southampton Central
2.30p.m.	Alton	Eastleigh
2.58p.m.	Southampton Central	Portsmouth
4.05p.m.	Andover	Romsey
4.09p.m.	Eastleigh	Southampton Terminus
4.22p.m.	Eastleigh	Romsey
4.35p.m.	Portsmouth	Salisbury
4.57p.m.	Fareham	Southampton Central
5.05p.m.	Romsey	Eastleigh
5.18p.m.	Southampton	Alton
5.32p.m.	Eastleigh	Portsmouth
5.25p.m.	Southampton Terminus	Portsmouth
6.03p.m.	Portsmouth	Southampton Central
6.15p.m.	Southampton	Portsmouth

6.45p.m.	Portsmouth	Southampton Central
6.47p.m.	Waterloo	Southampton
7.30p.m.	Alton	Winchester
7.40p.m.	Eastleigh	Portsmouth
7.45p.m.	Portsmouth	Andover
8.03p.m.	Portsmouth	Eastleigh
9.39p.m.	Eastleigh	Salisbury
9.46p.m.	Portsmouth	Southampton Terminus
10.00p.m.	Southampton Terminus	Portsmouth
10.33p.m.	Winchester	Southampton Central
8.28p.m.	Salisbury	Portsmouth
Freight		
5.12a.m.	Fratton	Netley
7.07a.m.	Eastleigh	Chichester
7.46a.m.	Fratton	Cosham
10.42a.m.	Fareham	Cosham
11.05a.m.	Fareham	Bevois Park
1.31p.m.	Basingstoke	Eastleigh
4.47p.m.	Havant	Eastleigh
8.25p.m.	Eastleigh	Chichester
9.50p.m.	Eastleigh	Fratton

Some of the times are in not in strict chronological order but these are copied exactly as written.

Another stored loco, this time No. 722 (another 'T9') and this time at the rear of Eastleigh shed on 12 November 1949. Converted in September 1947, the frames of this engine at least would live on for a further eight years under sister engine No. 732. This was one of four converted engines seen by an observer at Eastleigh in the month conversion had taken place. Notice in the background just above the tender an end brick wall clearly of recent construction and very similar in outline to the boiler/pump house seen earlier. It is possible this was the second boiler house at Eastleigh, which was to provide a steam 'ring-main' around the inside of the shed for lighting up purposes. *Bluebell Railway Archives*

A selection of loco duties and believed be from November 1947. (There were certainly more, especially for the 'N15' and 'WC' types.) In all cases these are the loco duties and they do not necessarily mean the same crew remained with the engine throughout its turn. (Three other duties are partly reported but these are mostly illegible on the original paperwork and consequently have not been copied. One is also the working to Winchester Cheesehill on which the previously reported failure occurred.):

Eastleigh Duty No. 312

(Q1 class – oil burner) [– likely meaning either/or]		
Alternate date with 277 duty.		
Loco Yard		6.35a.m.//A
(Via Southampton Junction)		
XX	Eastleigh	7.07a.m.F
8.05a.m.	Havant	9.15a.m.F
Saturdays excepted.		
9.35a.m.	Chichester	XX //
(or as ordered)		
XX	Eastleigh Loco	
Saturday only		
9.35a.m.	Chichester	XX //
XX	Fratton Loco	12.03p.m.//
12.13p.m.	Portsmouth & Southsea	12.33p.m.P
1.44p.m.	Southampton Town	2.38p.m.
2.45p.m.	Southampton Central	
	Freight shunting 2.55p.m.	
	Until	3.55p.m.
	Southampton Central	3.55p.m.F
4.0p.m.	Bevois Park	XX //
XX	Southampton Docks	5.34p.m.F
7.26p.m.	Eastleigh	XX //
XX	Loco Yard	

Eastleigh Duty No. 290

(T9 – oil burner).		
	Loco Yard	4.25a.m.
XX	Eastleigh	4.52a.m.
	(news)	
5.33a.m.	Portsmouth Harbour	XX //
XX	Fratton Loco	8.30a.m.//
8.40a.m.	Portsmouth & Southsea	9.03a.m.P
10.08am	Winchester	10.45a.m.P
11.19a.m.	Southampton Town	11.57a.m.
	(vans)	
12.11p.m.	Eastleigh	XX //
XX	Loco Yard	
Saturdays excepted		
	Loco yard	3.50p.m.//
XX	Eastleigh	4.22p.m.P
4.57p.m.	Romsey	5.05p.m.P
5.23p.m.	Eastleigh	5.32p.m.P
6.19p.m.	Portsmouth & Southsea	
	Loco Yard	
	Portsmouth & Southsea	8.03p.m.P
8.52p.m.	Eastleigh	9.39p.m.P
10.31p.m.	Salisbury	XX //
	Loco Yard	

Eastleigh duty 277		
(N15 – oil burner)		
Alternate duties with 312 Duty		
	Eastleigh	4.55a.m. //
5.10a.m.	Southampton Town	6.00a.m.P
8.36a.m.	Waterloo	8.55a.m.//
9.10a.m.	Nine Elms	6.05p.m.//
6.30p.m.	Waterloo	6.47p.m. (Parcels)
8.53p.m.	Basingstoke	9.07p.m. (Parcels)
9.54a.m.	Eastleigh	10.10p.m. P.Q.
10.22p.m.	Southampton Town	XX //
XX	Eastleigh	

Another BR renumbering, 'T9' No. 121 at Eastleigh. This engine was part of the original allocation of five of the class based here. It was one of three converted 'officially' on the same day, 30 August 1947, and had its BR number added in June 1948. The view was taken on 4 September 1948, with less than a month to go before oil burning ceased. *Mike King collection*

This time it is 'L11' No. 155 in reasonable external condition – for an oil burner that is – and also in final form on 4 September 1948. Most, if not all, of the 4-4-0s had a basic framework supporting the electric generator fitted in the same place and which would have made the engine slightly heavier on one side. Converted to oil in October 1948, the generator was fitted at the same time. Note that the large white tank standing vertical behind the engine is nothing to do with the oil fuel and was instead for water softening. *Mike King collection*

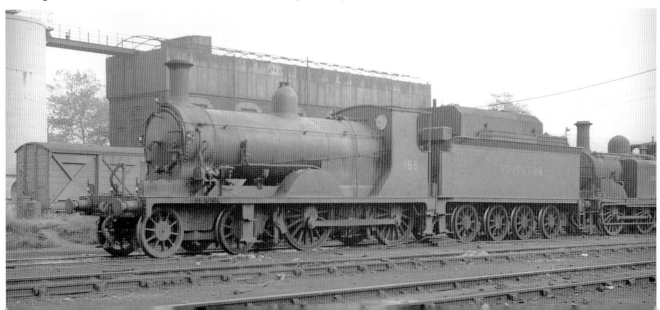

Eastleigh duty No. 319

(T9 class – oil burner)

	Eastleigh Loco	5.15a.m.//
5.35a.m.	Winchester	6.36a.m.P
7.11a.m.	Southampton Town	8.02a.m.P
(6.45a.m. ex Andover Junction)		
9.09a.m.	Portsmouth & Southsea	XX //
XX	Fratton	11.05a.m. (Vans)
12.06p.m.	Eastleigh	XX //
XX	Eastleigh Loco	4.00p.m.//
Xx	Eastleigh	4.30p.m.E
	(light engine on Saturdays)	
4.40.p.m.	Southampton Town	5.25p.m.P
6.37p.m.	Portsmouth & Southsea	
	Loco Yard.	
	Portsmouth & Southsea	7.45p.m.P
10.04p.m.	Andover Junction	XX //
XX	Loco Yard.	
	Stable for No. 271 duty next day	

Eastleigh duty No. 316

(T9 class – oil burner).

	Loco Yard	8.30a.m.//
XX	Eastleigh	9.03a.m.P
(8.32a.m. ex Romsey)		
9.53a.m.	Portsmouth & Southsea	
	Loco Yard	
	Portsmouth & Southsea	11.26a.m.P
1.38p.m.	Andover Junction	
(C. shunting until 2.00p.m.)		
	Andover Junction	2.00p.m.
Saturdays excepted		
Xx	Loco Yard	3.40p.m.//
	Andover Junction	4.05p.m.P
4.50p.m.	Romsey	5.35p.m.//
5.53p.m.	Eastleigh loco	
Saturdays only		
XX	Loco Yard	2.55p.m.//
XX	Andover Junction	
	Freight shunting	
	Andover Junction	4.50p.m.F
4.55p.m.	Andover Town	
	Freight shunting	
	Andover Town	6.10p.m.F
6.15p.m.	Andover Junction	
(Freight and Coaching shunting until 12.00midnight		
	Coaching hunting 1 hour	
	Freight shunting 4 hours 45 minutes	
	Andover Junction	12.00 midnight
XX	Loco Yard	
Stable for No. 272 duty Monday.		

Fratton duty 361

(T9 class oil burner)

	Fratton	6.25a.m.??A
6.35a.m.	Portsmouth & Southsea	6.55a.m.P
8.06a.m.	Southampton Central	++//
	Northam Yard (Trip)	
	Southampton Quay	++//
	Southampton Town	12.45p.m.P (SX)
	Illegible	12.53p.m.P (SO)
2.04p.m.	Portsmouth & Southsea	
SX		
2.07p.m.	Portsmouth & Southsea	++//
SO		
	Fratton Loco	9.15p.m.//
9.25p.m.	Portsmouth & Southsea	9.46p.m.P
10.54p.m.	Southampton Town	11.30p.m.//
11.45p.m.	Eastleigh	
Detach coaches off 11.10p.m. ex Sarum and attach		
To 1.10.a.m. ex Southampton Terminus.		
	Eastleigh	1.46a.m.P
2.28a.m.	Portsmouth & Southsea	++//
	Fratton Loco	

Fratton duty No. 362

(U class oil burner)

	Fratton	5.53a.m.//
6.03a.m.	Portsmouth & Southsea	6.23a.m.P
7.40a.m.	Southampton T	8.07a.m.E (SX)
8.26a.m.	Eastleigh	9.40a.m. F
	(start 9.50a.m. SO)	
11.04a.m.	Fratton Yard	++//
	Fratton Loco	3.50p.m.?? A
4.02p.m.	Havant	4.47p.m. F
6.27p.m.	Eastleigh	++//
	Loco Yard	7.55p.m.//
	Eastleigh	8.25p.m.F
10.23p.m.	Chichester	++//
	Fratton Loco	

No. 731 ('T9') at Eastleigh on 20 September 1947. Two tool boxes will be noted along with tubular access ladders to the rear of the tender but as yet no electric lighting – this was added on 30 January 1948. (By September the following year, the engine was observed at Fratton and then in the same month on LSWR coaching stock at Eastleigh in company with coal-burning 'L11' No. 151.) The photographer's notes refer to the image being taken on an official shed visit (SLS perhaps) at which Henry Casserly was also present. *Frank Foote courtesy Mike King*

'T9' No. 280 at Fratton in September 1948; would it in fact ever run again? We know for certain not all the converted engines were active simultaneously. Note the two tool boxes, both with the lids open. *Frank Foote courtesy Mike King*

Dwarfed somewhat by the tender of the Bulleid in front, this is 'L11' No. 172 at Eastleigh and also affording a good view of the framing for the generator. A fire extinguisher is also visible to the right of the toolbox. The headcode could indicate a light engine move between Eastleigh and Portsmouth. This was one of just two from the class – the other was No. 170 – that were based at Fratton. *Amyas Crump*

Fratton Duty No. 364

(T9 or L12 oil burner)		
	Fratton	7.00a.m.//
7.10a.m.	Portsmouth & Southsea	7.29a.m.P
9.19a.m.	Salisbury	++//
	Loco Yard	
	Salisbury	
(8.10.a.m. ex Bristol)		
12.31p.m.	Portsmouth & Southsea	++//
	Fratton	4.05p.m.
4.15p.m.	Portsmouth & Southsea	4.35p.m.P
6.51p.m.	Salisbury	++//
	Loco Yard	7.40p.m.//
	Salisbury	8.28p.m.P
(4.35p.m. ex Cardiff)		
9.16p.m.	Eastleigh	9.28p.m.P
10.19p.m.	Portsmouth & Southsea	
	c-shunting until 4.20a.m.	
	Portsmouth & Southsea	4.20a.m.//
4.25a.m.	Fratton	

Key:
A – Engine prepared
F – Freight
P – Passenger
++ – Time uncertain
// – Light Engine
The XX symbol is not explained

Without attempting to analyse the minutiae of every working, a few points do stand out. Firstly, that for most turns more than one loco crew would have been involved. Next, there are some tender-first workings involved. it would also appear there were a number of light-engine movements – more so it seems that would normally be the case and perhaps explained by the engine workings for the oil burners being limited so far as their sphere of operation was concerned. Finally, it will be noted there were lay-overs at both Salisbury and more noticeably at Nine Elms, in the latter case for almost nine hours from 9.10a.m. to 6.05p.m. Clearly the engine concerned would have its fire let out for this time and only relit ready for the evening return. So does this mean a trained Eastleigh crew arrived almost mid-afternoon or was there someone at Nine Elms with the necessary knowledge?

Another 'T9', this one No. 303, and with the wide cab and splashers. It also has an identical headcode to that seen previously and is seen sometime between September 1947 and February 1948 – the latter date when the generator was fitted. *Jeremy Staines*

5
From everything to nothing

The formal order to cease work on converting engines and the installations themselves was from 8 January 1948 – officially referred to as a 'postponement' but as we know, it would never start again. Taking a snapshot at that point, we know Fratton was operational and 'virtually complete' (what may still have been required is not mentioned) whilst in general terms Eastleigh was considered to be 99 per cent complete – slightly optimistic perhaps – as some (unspecified) work was still needed to make the building watertight. (We believe this at least was done.) In reality the 99 per cent probably referred to the boiler/pump house building with work on the pumps at 60 per cent and 72 per cent for the tanks. The figures for Exmouth Junction were respectively 85, 25 and 95 per cent.

Ironically, the financial calculations were such that all three depots could have been finished for want of a further £20,000

'L11' No. 155 recoded on 28 May 1950, so clearly stored but minus any chimney protection. Officially all the oil burners were withdrawn at the start of October 1948 but as we know there were occasional movements for a few days subsequently, while No. 34036 is another story.
W. Gilburt/R.K. Blencowe

in total. A further £9,000 would be needed to undertake work at the 'topping up' points where nothing had been started.

There had, in fact, been a hint of this 'postponement' back in September 1947 – just four months earlier. Pointedly, on 23 September the REC directed that '… the conversion of further engines to burn oil be suspended for the present'. This statement appears not to have been broadcast outside at the time – if at all – and also goes to explain why the earlier table of figures for conversions (*see* p.50) stops abruptly the following month. (The October conversions were obviously already under way on 23 September.) So, was this 23 September decision directly related to what would follow in January? Possibly yes and indeed that is the most likely conclusion to draw – the government having realised the financial consequences of their decision to commence the conversion programme were not to the country's advantage after all. But we should also consider there may also have been other factors that we should consider and these were simply the rate of progress of the ground installation and similarly with the engine conversions, both dependent upon labour and materials. Again, our 'chicken and egg' situation of not wanting to have converted engines standing idle and so unavailable to traffic.

'No' No. 1831 alongside the coaling stage at Eastleigh – it certainly would not have needed servicing here. The comment earlier in the text about the oil burner being enveloped in flames after dripping oil was ignited by hot ash in this area also just goes to show that the system for dealing with oil burners 'coming on shed' was not really organised as the disposal area was 100 per cent planned for coal burners. This was seen sometime after September 1947 and January 1948, and with a headcode indicating a main line working. *S.C. Nash/Stephenson Locomotive Society*

Not surprisingly, this was also the time the monthly progress reports ceased as well. At the same time it was reported the government asked for the costs to restore the engines back to coal burning, which would be borne by central government except, it was stated, the original five conversions undertaken by the GWR – and presumably their original fixed installations. (Poor GWR, we might actually feel for them here. In the vanguard of the idea, and it was of course from them and their experiences that the government instructed the whole scheme go ahead. Now they were being financially penalised for something that was not their fault.)

Little else of any consequence is then reported until 8 June 1948, when at a meeting held this time at the Marylebone headquarters, Roland C. Bond presided over a meeting of Chairman and senior officers of the regions. Messrs Burow (CME) and Taylor (CCE) represented the SR.

Bond made brief mention of the government's intention to abandon the coal to oil conversion scheme. The Railway Executive had previously informed the British Transport Commission that so far as could be foreseen at the present time none of the new oil fuel depots would need to be retained. Because of the specialist equipment it was not thought possible to use any in connection with any future diesel locomotives schemes.

A summary was also given that stated so far ninety-three locomotives had been converted by the four railways and the intention of the Railway Executive was that that they should

continue in operation during the summer traffic. At the end of this period they would probably be converted back to coal. (I am not sure why the report used the word 'probably'.) The regions would be asked to submit a list of locomotives presently running on oil indicating when they would normally be due for repairs in shops so that consideration could be given to a programme for conversion. It seems as if the railways were themselves a little sure which way the wind was blowing for they asked a message be passed on to government for the cost of retaining the depot buildings and installations on a care and maintenance basis – painting oil tanks and steelwork, etc, to be covered.

Less than two months later, on 28 July 1948, an official notice was issued by the Southern Region (and presumably the other regions) for all the oil-burning locos to be stored 'serviceable' at end of the summer. Meanwhile, the region had stated the one 'WC' converted, No. 34019, 'cannot be used to good effect' and should be converted at first opportunity. This was agreed by Marylebone, while the five members of the 'N15' type would be reconverted as they went through shops in the normal way, although if this was not due they might be dealt with as a special case.

Around the same time, the SR reported that applications had been received from various (unspecified) sources to acquire the tanks, while consideration was being given to taking up the track at the oil depots with a view to assisting the engineer's relaying programme.

And so to 'the big one', No. 34019 *Bideford* seen here in fresh malachite with BR number but retaining its 'Southern' roundel on the smokebox. Due to the shape of the coal bunker, it can be difficult to confirm views of the engine are actually with an oil tank but we are 99.9 per cent certain it is seen here in this condition. John Bailey noted this engine three times. Firstly, on 10 June 1947, when it arrived at Eastleigh shed, the fire was disposed of and it was then steamed into the shed and placed, as he puts it, 'on a dead line' for the engine to cool. He next saw it on 14 July in the works yard, converted but out of steam. Finally, on 25 July, it was noted on trial; we may assume he means at Eastleigh but this is not confirmed. Co-incidentally, the Southern Railway/Region eventually built 110 of these 'Light Pacifics', exactly the same number of engines the Southern Railway had intended to convert to burn oil. *Jeremy Staines*

Slightly earlier in time, the same engine carrying its original SR number 21C119 and clearly showing the results of an oil fire. It would be both unfair and unwise to blame either the oil bath or the oil fuel, although clearly some remedial work was required and was likely the time the repaint seen in the previous view was carried out. *S.C. Townroe/R.K. Blencowe*

The Depots and Refuelling

Before speaking fully of contractions and conversions, we should deal in more detail with the oil fuel installations and the locomotives themselves, although these have, of course, been illustrated previously – again an example of the proverbial 'chicken and egg' scenario.

Hugh Abbinnett has already referred to the physical installation built at Eastleigh. There exists but one illustration of this, taken by Stephen Townroe, which shows the building complete but not the tanks, although the cradles for these are visible on the right-hand side of the building. Abbinnett at least does tell us the tanks were installed on their respective cradles later and, with a capacity of 40,000 gallons, were the largest intended supply point on the Southern, sufficient to fuel twenty-five tender tanks each of 1,600-gallon capacity. Within the structure were the boiler(s), no doubt actually installed with the structure built around it. Using knowledge of the Exmouth Junction installation, we know that at the latter the storage tanks at least were erected and of 25,000-gallon capacity, and according to later correspondence at least one

building was also erected, although there are no illustrations of the latter. An unnamed correspondent in the *Railway Observer* speaks of two former 'D1' boilers intended to be installed to supply steam being sent to Exmouth Junction and we may then conclude that a similar arrangement was installed at both Eastleigh and Fratton. Two boilers would also allow one to be in use continually.

As the main storage tanks were outside, the intention was for these to be lagged with asbestos but we do not know if at Fratton especially this was actually carried out. Again, this is where the lack of technical information comes to the fore. From the 1946 pamphlet *Oil-Burning Locomotive* referred to in the bibliography but which refers exclusively to the involvement of the GWR, it indicates a steam pipe was passed through the storage tanks in order to keep the contents viscous. Possibly this involved additional coils within as well. We know, of course, the oil was pumped as required in its viscous state to the locomotive tender, where again there were steam pipes/coils to maintain fluidity, but does that mean the delivery pipes from the storage tanks to the filling points were similarly heated – lagged certainly?

The Eastleigh fuelling point on 11 September 1948, hardly synonymous with the expectations of Hugh Abbinnett and his colleagues just a year before. Former 'D1' 0-4-2T No. 700S, before this No. 2244 and before that LBSCR No. 244 *Hassocks*, is seen on the fuel point and retaining some of the various embellishments from its Second World War fire-fighting days – the pump at the rear of the bunker especially. In fire-fighting guise it had been able to pump a ton of water per minute but, not withstanding the viscosity of warm oil being far better than the cold product, the thickness even of warm oil would have meant the pumping output would have been far less in practice. The engine could also no longer move under its own power but steam was generated to pass through an adjacent tank car – as here – to maintain the oil in a fluid state; to provide steam to the atomiser of an engine 'cold' and needing to be lit up and, of course, also to pump the actual oil itself. For this reason alone, a goodly supply of coal was required (the shovel will be noted). We are not informed how long these various tasks might have taken.

From the front we see the same engine and really looking in a pitiful state; spectacle plate glass missing and it appears various items of detritus have been abandoned on the cab roof. The red lamp on the front is also apparent – a form of health and safety at least if refuelling was necessary in the dark. From this angle, too, we may see the oil delivery hose at the front.

As a temporary refuelling arrangement, two former 'D1' 0-4-2T locos that had previously been fitted with pumps as mobile fire-fighting engines in the Second World War were adapted for oil pumping heating. Hugh Abbinnett also referred to this earlier, No. 2244 originally in use at Fratton before moving to Eastleigh, where it was noted by John Bailey on 12 April 1947 and subsequently photographed by Henry Casserley performing this duty on 20 May 1947. We may therefore conclude that both No. 740 and No. 305 were first bunkered at Fratton prior to that depot becoming operational.

Still dealing with the 'D1s', in its new role, No. 2244 was later renumbered 700S. With the continuation of 'experimental' work involving No. 34036, No. 700S outlived the operational life of all the other oil burners and was, in theory at least, 'on the books' until withdrawn in May 1949.

A second engine of the same type, No. 2284, was similarly adapted (what these actual adaptations/modifications were is not known) and worked at Fratton at some stage with the number '701S'. It was lettered 'Oil Pump No. 2'. Whether 700S was similarly lettered is not referred to. What we do know is that on 10 December 1947, No. 701S commenced the long slow journey from Fratton towards Exmouth Junction, being hauled by coal-fired 'T9' No. 401 on the first part of the trip as far as

Salisbury. Towing was necessary as the two pumping 'D1s' were incapable of movement under their own power. It was noted as having arrived at Exmouth Junction by 13 December.

Another no doubt slow tow back to Eastleigh ensued a few months later as on 15 April 1948 No. 701S was back at Eastleigh – perhaps as a temporary stand-in for No. 2244. It would later move to Nine Elms, where it was still extant until officially withdrawn in December 1951 but by then in poor external condition and unlikely to have served any useful purpose other than cluttering up space since it left Hampshire. Assuming these dates together with that of the accompanying Casserley image to be correct, this means that for a time at least, both the oil pump engines were at Eastleigh. Despite Bulleid's earlier minuted comments made sometime in late January 1947 that five former 'fire-pump' engines were available for conversion, these would be the only two so dealt with.

A third 'D1', No. 2361, was scheduled to be adapted for oil pumping but the work was not carried out. Both 700S and 701S were coal fired, a spare fireman being despatched to attend to their needs. When attached to a tank wagon, the 'D1' was kept in steam so the oil in the tank wagon might be warmed via the engine steam heat connection.

Other than at Fratton, the permanent installations at Eastleigh and Exmouth Junction were never operational, hence the need for the 'D1s'. But Eastleigh came perhaps closer to (partial) completion than was realised for on 9 March 1948 Bulleid reported that in order to retain work for the thirty-one locomotives already equipped it would be necessary to complete one storage tank, erect one pump, one boiler and one fuelling arm together with the necessary pipework. He reported the present position as being; tanks 94 per cent complete, pumps 75 per cent, boilers and flues 50 per cent and pipe gantries and fuelling arms 15 per cent. We are also given some very useful information that, as planned, the completed station would have consisted of three tanks, five pumps, four boilers *and* three pipe gantries and fuelling arms.

At this stage we might refer again to the memories of John Click, who comments on the oil-burning scheme thus, 'The government scheme to oil fire 1,019* steam locomotives, which OVB was very keen on and got on with quickly, came to nothing. It wonderfully rejuvenated the T9s: I only rode on the one, No. 288, but it was a revelation. This one, and the 'small hopper' next to it, both enjoyed a brief life with this new fire in their bellies, but it didn't last long enough.'

A little later in his memoirs, Click talks of a time when he had 'climbed the ladder' and was now the Assistant Works Manager at Eastleigh. It may be unrelated to the period 1945–51 but as it refers briefly to an oil burner we include it if for nothing but slight amusement:

'As if it were an offering from the steam locomotive gods, my phone rang one day and a voice from "222" asked if we at Eastleigh would accept a War Department 2-10-0 from Longmoor in need of a general repair. I never turned work away, but there would be problems. "They want it converted to oil firing, as well," the voice went on. Needless to say, I jumped at it but didn't say why. Next day, when Manager Ellis returned, he was less than pleased. I had privately been looking out whatever records there were from the oil-firing period, I never quite made Harry Frith an "accessory" but he and I saw more than usual of each other when "Kitchener" was completed.'

[Clearly now referring to an unlocated photograph he adds:]

'Here we are at Fareham, in the bay, after our first and surprisingly disappointing test run, light engine. The public address had just crackled and delivered the following rather Rev. Awdrey-like message, "You big blue engine: you are not to go." Control had caught up with us: "Go on Harry, see what's up with them." I don't know what he told "them" but we went home.'

[This whole episode asks more questions than it answers, although it does tell us there *were* records at Eastleigh! The temptation is to speculate but under the circumstances this would not be the best course of action and instead without J.G.C. or Harry Frith, both no longer with us, to clear up ambiguity little more is able to be said.]

So we return to the converted 'N15' engines, commencing with No. 740. John Bailey first records having seen it at Eastleigh on 2 April 1947 but without further comment.

Having undoubtedly though served its purpose as a training engine, by August 1947 *Merlin* had a regular turn working the 4.52a.m. Eastleigh to Portsmouth and return 9.00a.m. Portsmouth–Winchester, returning thence to Eastleigh with empty stock. Only a limited amount of work, while any additional schedule for the remainder of the day is not reported.

All five of the converted 'N15' engines were based at Eastleigh with duties that also eventually included the 7.20a.m. Eastleigh to Waterloo, returning with 11.30a.m. Waterloo–Bournemouth. Again, we do not know if an engine change occurred on the down run at Eastleigh or if the 'King Arthur' worked through to Bournemouth, and if so how it returned to Eastleigh. Any conclusions are not helped as there is no apparent information on fuel consumption. With the emergency standby tanks never brought into use, no topping up would have been possible at Nine Elms or Bournemouth, etc.

Subsequently, and as confidence grew, so the sphere of activities widened and the class were reported as working (unspecified) fast passenger services from Waterloo to Salisbury, the 5.05p.m. Bournemouth West–Waterloo and 6.47p.m. Waterloo–Bournemouth parcels. There is also a *Railway Observer* report of an unidentified member taking the through Bournemouth to Birkenhead service as far as Oxford, which was the usual limit for SR engines working on to the GWR/WR. (GWR oil-burning types, certainly an example of a 'Castle', 'Hall' and a 2-8-0, were also known to have reached Salisbury on trains from Bristol/Westbury.)

As is also apparent from the illustrations, most of the images show the 'oilers' either static or stored after the end of the scheme. In a similar way, those few that do record trains or engines away from Eastleigh/Fratton depict the 4-4-0 types and we have just the single image of one of the 4-6-0s in revenue-earning service.

Upon restoration to coal fuel, No. 752 (we think) at least retained its electric lighting, whether this was for the remainder of its operational life is not confirmed.

Probably the last active member of the converted 'King Arthur' class was No. 745, which arrived at Waterloo on 2 October 1948 at the head of a relief service from Bournemouth. That was also the last time an oil-fired steam engine would ever been seen at the terminus. Upon its return to Eastleigh it was on paper at least placed in store (in reality taken immediately into works) as it is interesting to note that, again on paper, the same date is given for its reconversion back to burn coal.

The fact that no article or much information on the SR conversions has been located in the regular periodicals – technical and enthusiast – has already been mentioned, and yet in the *Meccano Magazine* for September 1947 (page 356) a single page piece by 'Shed Superintendent' entitled 'Have you ever thought about this? Oil Firing of Locomotives' appeared. 'Shed Superintendent' was a pen name used by S.C.

---

* Contemporary magazine sources quote the intended number to have been 1,229, so JGC's number may have been a simple misprint.

We now have three views showing the actual refuelling of a 'T9' – number not confirmed – but on the basis that the photographer's date is correct, 20 May 1947, it can only be No. 305, which was converted in January 1947. No. 2244 will certainly be in steam and pumping from the tank wagon behind to the locomotive tender tank. Clearly in the case of the latter, this was 'splash filling', hence it is no wonder the man on the tender is wearing overalls; the man in the cab of No. 2244 is similarly well protected. Might the bin on the right contain sand? When the engine required coal, it was refuelled from another engine on an adjacent track while water was obtained from the standpipe nearby and which probably determined where refuelling would take place. *H.C. Casserley*

Townroe for various articles, this piece illustrated with one of his photographs showing the cab and footplate of the first 'King Arthur' conversion.

Although clearly aimed at the younger enthusiast, it nevertheless contains useful information not sourced from elsewhere:

'The conversion of a number of locomotives to oil firing, as announced by British Railways last year, is not of course a difficult undertaking as far as the locomotives themselves are concerned, for this system of firing was in the experimental stage 50 years ago and has since been perfected.

'Fairly elaborate ground installations at the Locomotive Depots must, however be completed before the locomotives can be brought into regular service. Fuel oil is a dark, treacly substance that will only flow readily when warm. This means that the storage tanks and pipe lines must be heated and the fuel tanks on the tenders of the engines as well.

'At each Depot installation a stationary boiler is required, not only to heat the tanks but also to provide a supply of steam to each engine that requires to be lit up from cold.

'On an oil-fired engine the burner, fixed at the front of the firebox under the brick arch, takes the form of a tray, over which passes a jet of steam. Fuel oil is allowed to trickle on to the tray and directly it does so it is whisked off by the steam jet, which then becomes an inflammable mixture of steam and oil mist. When ignited, this jet is a sheet of flame, roaring in the firebox like a giant blowlamp. The pressure of steam at the jet and the rate of flow of the oil are controlled by vales on the fireman's side of the footplate and in the illustration the necessary fittings can be seen on the right-hand side. The oil control and damper control are both on pillars. Six small hand wheels adjust the steam supply to the burner, blower, tank warmer, etc.

'The normal firehole door is locked, as it will be understood from the foregoing remarks that the flame is directed rearwards towards the firehole door, and it is not safe to open it while the jet is alight. A small mica window is fitted to the door, through which the enginemen can observe the flame inside the firebox.

'Control of the burner is a matter of training, although once the burner has been correctly proportioned to the design of engine, proper combustion occurs pretty well throughout the range of oil adjustments, and on the road little more is necessary than to vary the oil supply with the rate that the engine is working. This needs considerable skill because the fireman must anticipate his driver's action all the time, turning on 'the gas' well in advance of steam requirements and shutting down directly the throttle is closed. The fireman must also take care to avoid excessive smoke, but if the burner is correctly set in the workshops, and the dampers properly adjusted, smoke is barely perceptible at full load and any smoke will disappear when the engine has warmed up to its task. The consumption of oil is 5–6 gallons to the mile under load, and sufficient fuel is carried for a 250-mile journey, with the standard equipment now in process of being fitted to main line engines.

'This consumption may appear heavy, but very little oil is used when idle, whereas a coal-burning engine has a fire on the grate all the time. Other advantages include rapid refuelling and a complete absence of ashes in the smoke-box or ashpan.'

We turn now to the smaller conversions, starting with the various 4-4-0 types converted to oil, and represented by three types. Numerically the largest number from any class were the thirteen members of the 'T9' class. All of these conversions were carried out at Eastleigh in 1947 and it will be noted that with the single exception of the 'training' engine, No. 305, all the work was undertaken in August and September 1947. (There had been the intention to convert a second 'T9' fairly rapidly to fulfil a similar familiarisation role at Exmouth Junction. Engines of the class were based at the depot as well as regularly working to the proposed emergency fuelling points planned west of Exeter. For reasons that are not explained, this was not done at this time.)

There is little mention about issues with the converted engines, excepting of course John Click's praise for them and, at the opposite end of the spectrum, Abbinnett's comment on the leaking tubes of another. Piecing together odd notes from the *Railway Observer* together with those of John Bailey plus photographic evidence, it appears that once released from works they spent only a very limited time at Eastleigh being run-in/trialled on local van and goods services, before being despatched, if appropriate, to Fratton or amalgamated into the general loco pool at Eastleigh. Two examples, Nos. 113 and 280, at least were not only converted but also had a clean and repaint, so these may have received additional mechanical work at the same time as the conversions.

Once all had been converted, the initial allocation of the 'T9' 'oilers' was:

Fratton: Nos. 113, 114, 115, 118, 280, 303, 305, 314.

Eastleigh: Nos. 121, 286, 713, 722, 731.

	Date converted to oil (none reverted to coal)	Withdrawn	Disposal
113	Sept. 1947	May 1951	To store at Fratton from 6-10-48. Moved to Elh. By 6-6-51.
114	Sept. 1947	May 1951	To store at Fratton from 6-10-48. Moved to Elh. By 6-6-51.
115 BR No. 30115 Jun. 1948*	Aug. 1947	May 1951	To store 6-10-48. Cut up Elh. w/e 19-5-51.
118	Aug. 1947	Apr. 1951	Cut up w/e 26-5-51.
121 BR No. 30121 Jun. 1948*	Aug. 1947	May 1951	Cut up w/e 14-4-51.
280	Sept. 1947	May 1951	
286 BR No. 30286 May 1948*	Sept. 1947	Apr. 1951	Cut up Elh. w/e 2-6-51.
303	Sept. 1947	Jun. 1951	
305	Jan. 1947	Apr. 1951	
314	Sept. 1947	May 1951	Cut up Elh. w/e 9-6-51.
713	Sept. 1947	Apr. 1951	Cut up Elh. w/e 12-4-51.
722	Sept. 1947	Apr. 1951	Cut up Elh. w/e 26-4-51.
731	Sept. 1947	May 1951	
732		Oct. 1959	Stored at Eastleigh for conversion but had not been taken into works by the time the scheme was abandoned. (had run with the frames of No. 722 since Apr. 1951.)
733		Apr. 1952	Stored at Eastleigh for conversion but had not been taken into works by the time the scheme was abandoned.

* BR number added to cabsides but only painted on to buffer beam – no smokebox plate carried.

All the engines of this class were fitted with generators and electric lighting, although exactly when this took place is the subject of some debate. What we may say with certainty is that it was likely a retrospective fitting subject to the availability of the actual equipment. All the class also ran with 4,000 double-bogie tenders and, to quote Bradley, '... fitted precariously in the coal space'. Two of the engines – not specified – had arrived in works with six-wheel tenders but these were exchanged for the larger type from 'S11' class 4-4-0s Nos 395 and 396. (None of the 'S11' class were converted for oil.)

It is believed this remained constant throughout their oil-burning lives.

In service and being, of course, smaller engines, their sphere of operation was understandably less and the general duties undertaken were on a variety of local workings in the Portsmouth, Southampton, Eastleigh and Salisbury areas. One or more are also known to have ventured to Basingstoke and also to Alton.

As an example of their work, No. 305 (Fratton) was soon working the 7.46am Eastleigh to Bournemouth, returning with

Lesser quality but here we have the man on top of the tender tank – slippery perhaps in the event of spilt oil? Otherwise the conversation continues. The handbrake on the oil tank wagon – the number of which we can now see as 2761 – is also applied. It is a slightly strange place to leave a loco boiler on the right. Eastleigh shed would certainly not have the facility to effect a boiler change such as this, so might it even be a boiler that has arrived for installation in one of the boiler houses? The tank cars used were under the control of the Air Ministry and could carry 17 tonnes. They were, though, limited to a 14T load due to avoid exceeding the maximum axle loading. All were steam heated. *H.C. Casserley*

the 11.48am ex Bournemouth West. Normally the latter was a lightly loaded train but when especially strengthened to 300 tons, No. 305 still coped with steam to spare. One specific and dated turn was on 28 June 1947, when the same engine was seen piloting No. 21C150 and also recorded between Salisbury and Southampton with the through Plymouth Brighton service. This particular working split at Southampton, with No. 305 taking the Portsmouth portion forward. On another occasion, No. 305 was reported as taking the through Bristol service from the Southern as far as Salisbury. As this had been the first conversion of the class, possibly information was being gleaned for future use.

John Bailey recounts being pulled by No. 713 between Romsey and Fratton on 20 September 1947 and while at Fratton saw another 'oiler', 'T9' No. 118, double heading with a coal-fired 'S11'.

In their converted form, the class were now not just free running but free steaming and capable as well, although with a tendency to set light to sleepers in sidings and stations – recall the oily residue that would accumulate on and in the vicinity of the sleepers whenever steam engines would stand regularly.

Officially the last day of oil working was specified as Saturday, 2 October 1948, when No. 280 was active between Southampton and Portsmouth, although five days later there is a reported sighting of No. 286 on a Portsmouth to Eastleigh local on Thursday, 7 October 1948. If accurate the reasons might be various, including the need perhaps to move the

engine to storage at Eastleigh, or a harassed shed foreman having nothing else at his disposal to work the service.

We now turn to the other 4-4-0 classes, again ex LSWR designs. The first and, as it turned out, solitary member of the 'D15' so altered was No. 463 in September 1947 (John Bailey has the actual date as being the 23rd), although the original intention had been to convert ten of the class. As with the 'T9' type and the 'N15' conversions, a single Mexican Trough-type burner was fitted and in this condition the engine was similarly first trialled on local services around Eastleigh. Electric lighting was fitted three months after the conversion, while No. 463 also retained its original six-wheel tender.

Once proven, No. 463 was both a regular and a popular performer on Portsmouth–Salisbury and also Eastleigh–Bournemouth–Weymouth turns. With the 'oilers' allocations based around Eastleigh and Fratton, we may reasonably assume the duties undertaken revolved (excepting Exmouth Junction, but see later) around the turns worked by Eastleigh and Fratton men. It would also be interesting to know if in converted condition it worked any of the Waterloo–Lymington summer Saturday trains, as was the case with the coal-burning engines of the same class. Despite its apparent success, it was laid aside in October 1948 and dumped at Eastleigh, although it remained 'on the books' until formerly withdrawn in November 1951.

The final 4-4-0 engines altered to burn oil were the eight members of the 'L11' class – ten had been scheduled for conversion.

	Date converted to oil (none reverted to coal)	Withdrawn	Disposal
148	Sept. 1947 elec. 11/47	Mar. 1952	Ashford
154	Oct. 1947 elec. 10/47	Mar. 1951	
155	Oct. 1947 elec. 10/47	Mar. 1951	
157	Oct. 1947 elec. 10/47	Mar. 1952	Ashford
170	Oct. 1947 elec. 1/48	Mar. 1952	Ashford
172	Sept. 1947 elec. 3/48	Jun. 1952	Ashford
411	Aug. 1947 elec. 3/48	Jun. 1952	
437	Jul. 1947 elec. 1/48	Jun. 1952	Ashford?

All had eight-wheel tenders and would receive an electric generator fitted on the left-hand framing alongside the firebox. None received a BR number.

With the exception of Nos 170 and 172 sent to Fratton, the remainder were at Eastleigh. The Fratton pair found employment on local goods and yard piloting, while the Eastleigh-based engines were used on passenger, van and goods duties to Portsmouth, Andover Junction, Salisbury, Fawley, Bournemouth and Alton.

Possibly the last operational member was No. 411, noted on a van train at Brockenhurst as late as 30 November 1947. Subsequent to this, the electric generators fitted to the engines of this class were removed and used to provide power for 'ship to shore' radios fitted to the USA tank engines, allowing communication between the footplate and the shunter.

Before dealing with the remainder of the conversions, it is worth mentioning that no members of the similar LSWR 4-4-0 'L12', 'K10' or 'S11' 4-4-0 classes were converted. The 'official' list does not mention these classes, so we may also take a moment to consider exactly why.

Possibly the answer is explained simply with perceived life expectancy. Indeed, so far as the 'L12' class is concerned all but two had gone by the end of 1951, the 'K10s' had similarly started to fall by the wayside from 1947 on, and the 'S11' class had also, with one exception, also disappeared by the end of 1951. Possibly it was felt the 'T9s' were likely to have a longer lifespan, although that was not to be the case for the coal-fired 'D15' and 'L11' engines.

We are now left with the two final types, the 'Moguls' and the 'Bulleids'.

	Date converted to oil	Back to coal
1625 (U)	Sept–Dec. 1947 Ashford. Elec. Gen. Feb.1948	Nov–Dec. 1948 at Ashford.
1629 (U)	Work on conversion started 12 Sept. 1947 at Ashford. Work cancelled and reverted to coal 26 Oct. 1947.	
1797 (U)	July–Oct. to oil. Converted at Ashford.	Nov–Dec. 1948 at Ashford.
1831 (N)	June–Sept. 1947 to oil. Converted at Ashford. Elec. Gen. Jan. 1948.	Nov–Dec. 1948 at Ashford.

All three retained six-wheel tenders but Nos. 1625 and 1629 swapped their 4,000-gallon water capacity tenders for 3,500 gallon types, which were deemed more suitable for taking an oil tank. In addition to No.1629 mentioned, other members of the 'U' class that been earmarked for conversion were Nos. 1613/16/35/37/38 and 1795/6.

According to Bradley, all three of the Moguls were first trialled around Ashford (again where was the fuel obtained from/delivered?), after which they made their way to Eastleigh. From the same source comes a confirmatory comment that any modifications and trials (for the Eastleigh conversions) were under the auspices of the running shed at Eastleigh without, it would appear, any formal help from the nearby works. Altogether very much a trial and error type of arrangement, but then so much steam engine development was still based on the similar lines.

While No. 1831 appears to have spent its time around Eastleigh, Nos. 1625/9 both made their way to Exmouth Junction, with No. 1625 working over the GWR main line to Plymouth on one of the regular crew familiarisation duties. We do not have dates for this sojourn in the west but it may well have coincided with the transfer of No. 701S to Exmouth Junction between December 1947 and April 1948.

The final two conversions on the Southern were both 'West Country' Pacifics, Nos 21C119 and 34036 out of an intended twenty to thirty members of the class. No. 21C119 was the first to be dealt with at Eastleigh between 16 and 26 July 1947. Again, a tender oil tank of 1,600-gallon capacity was fitted – as might be expected of welded construction – while a necessary further modification was the repositioning of the four vacuum brake cylinders so that there were now two each either side of the water filler, while tubular ladders were added at the rear to aid refuelling. (Tubular ladders were fitted to most if not all of the tenders carrying oil tanks.) The rocking grate was also removed as being superfluous. Neither of the Pacifics involved had need of further conversion as electric lighting provided from a steam generator was already the standard equipment on the class.

No. 21C119 was initially based at Eastleigh and employed on local passenger and goods duties before taking over a former 'King Arthur' turn: the 6.00a.m. Southampton–Waterloo and 11.30a.m. Waterloo–Bournemouth West. Unfortunately steam production was erratic – it was said (by Bradley) due to the presence of the thermic siphons getting in the way – and often resulted in plenty of black smoke and not a lot else. The addition of a second burner and a repositioning of the first was an improvement but the overall conclusion was that the Mexican Trough system was not entirely suitable to the design of the firebox. Following this modification and further trials from Eastleigh, No. 21C119 was despatched to Exmouth Junction, where it was employed on secondary passenger duties until restored to coal firing in September 1948 having run just 8,220 miles in six months.

We may question why, with steam production known to be shall we say less than ideal, the engine was entrusted to the more demanding duties mentioned? Possibly the answer was to make

It is not quite so certain what is going on here – it might even be a tea break! Assuming it is around the same time, the 'T9' appears to be in steam and with refuelling completed. Other than trips to other depots mentioned in the text, No. 700s (aka No. 2244) moved little around the Eastleigh site and was likely kept in almost continuous steam. So what might the arrangements have been for refuelling when it was required to undertake a boiler washout? The only feasible option would seem to be sending engines to Fratton for refuelling.

Tank engine and oil tanks outside No. 1 at Eastleigh, and this time awaiting the arrival of an engine to refuel. Spillage is all too apparent.

Here we see the same engine viewed from the opposite side and, it will be noted, carrying its 700S number. The view was taken on 4 September 1948, so they may well have renumbered the engine by now – unless there remained different identifications on either side! Unfortunately what we still do not have in clear shot are the hose connections between engines – the steam heat to the tank car would probably have been via the normal steam heat hose. Slightly less heat was produced by burning oil, 752ºF, which ignites at 850ºF but, as we know, this did not adversely affect performance. *Mike King*

'The one that got away' (well one of two actually). If we may count this as 'an engine', this 'T9' No. (30)732, together with No. 733, had been earmarked for conversion, although this never took place. The rest of the engine was combined with parts from No. 722 but retained the identity of 732 until withdrawn. It was seen at Eastleigh, and note in the background the two abandoned tender oil tanks.

a point, engineering or political, and with the lack of scientific testing facilities available to the railways generally the only way to do this was literally by said trial and error. Certainly there is no evidence to suggest that any of the oil-burning engines that operated on the Southern were ever coupled to a dynamometer car borrowed from one of the other regions or a more detailed analysis made of their abilities, but then in early 1948, with the regional locomotive exchanges taking place, perhaps it was simply that none were available. No oil-burning locomotive ever took part in these interchange trials either. But, the *Railway Observer* does make one tantalising suggestion around this time when again an unnamed correspondent mentions that interchange trials between a GWR oil-burning 'Castle' and 'the Southern …' are due to take place. No other information is forthcoming and the only other reference is a month or so later, when it is stated that the intended trials have not 'as yet' taken place. They never did.

So where might this story have come from? Most likely an enthusiast visitor to the shed at Eastleigh is the most probable answer. We should recall that at that time visits to railway installations by outsiders were commonplace. 'Assemble at 2.00pm on a particular Saturday outside the entrance to Eastleigh shed,' was a known example. A group would then be escorted in to take numbers, photographs and generally 'poke around'. In the course of this, and with human nature being what it is, some would no doubt speak to staff and thus rumours and stories would start. There could well have been some truth in the tale but now more than seventy years on it will likely always remain a rumour. Worth mentioning is that the late D.L. Bradley was one who would often join similar groups on both organised shed and works visits. To him number taking and photography was secondary to disappearing into dark offices with dusty files to record as much technical and historic information as he could – and we must be grateful he did – for so much paperwork involving what are now little-known or indeed forgotten work on steam was irretrievably lost in the 1960s.

The second 'West Country' conversion was all the more successful and involved sister engine No. 21C136, converted at Brighton as the last of the Southern oil burners before being released to traffic as No. s21C136 on 28 February 1948. Again the modifications previously outlined were carried out, although this time a single 'Swirlyflow' burner from Messrs Laidlaw-Drew (originally intended for 'T9' No. 314) was installed. The cost of this burner was put at £640.

Again working from Eastleigh on local duties, the steaming was once again initially poor, including a complete failure on several occasions (no further details are given) but once the (unspecified) teething troubles were overcome the engine was transformed. Indeed, so successful were the results that in addition to Waterloo turns, No. s21C136 was entrusted with the 'Atlantic Coast Express' as well as other West of England passenger and fitted freights.

As if to prove the ability of oil firing with No. s21C136, a trial run of twenty coaches was operated between Eastleigh and Weymouth, although probably the most remarkable result was when a train of eighteen brand new coaches *and* the dead weight of S15 No. 30510 was taken up the 1 in 250 gradient from Eastleigh to Basingstoke. Bradley states the S15 assisted only at the start and then became part of the trailing load. (The estimated weight of this train excluding No. s21C136 was in the order of 750 tons.) By the time Winchester was reached, just 7 miles from the start, the safety valves were lifting 'violently' and Basingstoke was reached with 265lb on the pressure gauge. We should not perhaps take this completely at face value as there are questions that would need to be asked first: what was the water level at Winchester, how much oil was burnt and did this special working keep to schedule? We also have no indication as to the speeds achieved, but even so it remains a credible performance and even if taken on its own showed that there was room for further development of the conventional steam locomotive; oil burning and the soon-to-be-developed Giesel ejector two obvious examples. Now what results might have been achieved with an oil-fired, Giesel-fitted 'Merchant Navy' years later?

The 'infamous' No. 34036 – the one engine certain people on the Southern Region seemed it hoped might not be noticed. Exactly how it managed to be kept running for so long has not been established, and we can only guess at who might have been responsible. It is seen here at Eastleigh with what will be a stack of firebricks behind the tender. As early as March 1947, the supply of firebricks was stated to be a problem, although the files do not indicate if this was the specific bricks for the oil burners or firebricks generally. Unlike with the 'Leader' later, which intentionally had a wall of firebricks added to the inside of the firebox and which would then collapse on a regular basis, there is no mention of what was a shorter wall of firebricks on the oil burners collapsing, although it must be stated that is not to say it did not happen. Later on matters had most certainly improved for, on 8 August 1947, the SR reported a stock of no fewer than 85,900 with another 3,000 on order – but we do not know if these were 'oil-burner' specific.

After this, the trials with No. s21C136 were deliberately prolonged but we know nothing of the form they took. What we do know is that, as an oil burner, it was to remain the longest-working SR engine with oil fuel as it was not reconverted to coal until October 1949. The official reason given is that information could be obtained in case the scheme should be revived in the future, but as previously discussed, there may have been different reasons … Even so, it performed a useful purpose of using up the remaining oil available both on site and from the tender tanks of the various stored engines.

Having been based at Eastleigh since April 1948, its time there finally ended when, as a coal-burning engine, it was allocated to Brighton on 5 January 1950.

Unfortunately, despite the promise shown on both the SR and also on the GWR, who were the only other company of the 'big four' to truly embrace the new fuel, the economic situation was if anything getting worse. Apart from any balance of payment issues, it seems ridiculous now to report that the Ministry of Transport appears not to have consulted the Treasury from the outset, with the result that funds were simply not available for the purchase of the necessary oil to enable the complete scheme to proceed.

Aside from coal, Britain had little to export at this time. Consumer goods were the requirement and these the UK were unable to provide in anything like the required volume – if at all. Rationing remained in the UK and in some cases would last until the early 1950s. It was a hard time for all, with food allowances cut still further on certain products with the understandable call from the public, 'Why, with the war well and truly, over are so many goods still unobtainable?' All this time the value of sterling against the dollar was falling, with the inevitable result that the pound was devalued by 30 per cent in September 1949. In numeric terms this meant a fall from $4.03 dollars to the pound to one of $2.80. The chance for any resumption of oil firing thus fell even further and with it the fate of the twenty-two Drummond 4-4-0s languishing at Eastleigh, Fratton and elsewhere was sealed. The only hope now was for a re-conversion back to coal but that, as we know, would never happen.

Meanwhile, back on what was now the Southern Region, instructions were issued that oil fuel operations were to cease. It is believed these came out in late September 1948 to take effect from Saturday, 2 October but, as reported, we know there was still the odd sporadic movement for a few days after. On that actual day an observer reported to the *Railway Observer* that Eastleigh played host to Nos 21C136, 148/54/5/7, 411/37/63, 713/22/45/8/9, 30121, 30286 and 700S, while apart from No. 280 mentioned earlier, No. 463 was also observed on a Southampton–Portsmouth service.

Within the CME's department decisions had been taken to restore the converted 'King Arthur', U, N, and 'West Country' conversions to coal as soon as possible, and we have seen from earlier that this took place from October 1948 onwards. The fate of the remaining twenty-two Drummond 4-4-0s, though, appears to have hung in the balance. Initially they were simply stored, some with the telltale sacking over the chimney top, but all still notionally 'on the books'. Indeed, if conversion had been

a simple task initially why not simply revert to coal? Clearly this was a consideration, confirmed by the length of time they remained 'intact' before withdrawal. We may only conclude that the decision as to a reversion to coal, a resumption of oil working, or withdrawal was not easy. Perhaps, in the opinion of the present writer, it was one that was simply put off time and time again. What we have no means of knowing is their mechanical/boiler-firebox condition. We know of at least one 'T9' that leaked badly from the tubes, so were others similarly poor? Had the sudden and intense heat associated with oil firing actually caused damage? In all likelihood the answer would be yes. Perhaps this fact alone, together with the limited life expectancy of the Drummond 4-4-0 design, was the real reason why coal burning did not recommence.

But this did raise a problem. With the twenty-two engines still notionally on the books, they formed part of the allocation to Eastleigh/Fratton considered necessary for covering all the respective depot's duties. There was thus a shortage, which was temporarily filled by borrowing ex SECR 4-4-0s. To be fair, none of these would have been in pristine condition either; an instruction to transfer an engine type to another depot was often manna from Heaven in allowing a shed master to rid himself of a lame duck. As we know, other coal-fired Drummond 4-4-0s were slowly falling by the wayside while this was going on, no doubt when major repairs became necessary and which were simply not justified on the basis of promised new engines on the horizon. It cannot have been easy for shed foremen like Mr Townroe and others. The solution was not to come until around 1954 with the arrival of the first of the BR Class 4 'Standard' types, which finally took over the duties of several of the former LSWR 4-4-0s.

With no financial information available, we cannot accurately estimate a full breakdown of costs incurred in the actual conversion process. Just thirty-two engines were converted out of the originally intended number, and there was the depot facilities, testing/crew training time, trials, etc. Then there were the indirect costs – moving engines around both during and subsequent to the programme. About the only things salvaged were some of the steam generators, twenty-nine fire pans (which were deemed as possibly useful on members of the 'U' and 'N' class engines), two tender tanks, and various spare nuts and bolts. The remainder – flanges, washers, some elements and five thermometers, together with various gauges – was simply scrap. (The official paperwork provides a spare parts list running to several closely typed pages of foolscap.)

One final point concerns the appearance at Eastleigh of two former LNWR (lettered LMS) tenders, each carrying what appears to be a 'standard' SR tender oil tank. How and why these arrived at Eastleigh is open to debate, one school of thought being they were originally used for diesel fuel oil, although they may also have been intended as an additional 'temporary' store for 'Bunker C' until it was required. Another view is that they were used as a supply for test purposes at the nearby Works. A similar tank appears in the background to views of 'Terriers' (coal burning) at Lancing, so did these tender(s) move about?

6
The final analysis

'T9' No. 113 at Eastleigh in 1947, probably fresh from conversion but awaiting electric lights. Apart from the experiment with the 'Swirlyflow'-type burner on No. 21C136, all the conversions country wide had the same type of burner, believed to have originated as a North British locomotive Company design. *Jeremy Staines collection*

At this stage the temptation has to be effect a brief conclusion casting blame mainly on the government of the day (and this refers to the generic word government rather than a specific political party), lack of 'joined up' discussion between departments, perhaps some individual civil servants, and overall a lack of foresight both practical and financial.

At which point we might end equally end proceedings, as indeed others have previously when referring to the 'debacle', 'shambles' and 'fiasco' – all of which have been words used to discuss the whole oil-burning exercise of the time and not just meaning the situation on the Southern.

Except, was it indeed a 'debacle' and was it actually over in October 1948? Some ninety-three Southern engines had been converted and no doubt useful information had been gained. Indeed, others some way away from the Southern clearly thought they might well profit from its experiences, witness a

letter written from the head office of the Hellenic State Railway (Athens) Mechanical and Rolling Stock on 28 May 1948 to the Southern Railway at Waterloo – we may forgive the Greeks for not knowing it was not in fact the Southern Region!

The letter referred back to the 30 August 1946 issue of the *Railway Gazette* and the proposed conversion of 1,217 engines to burn oil. In reality, of course, less than two years earlier but so much had occurred since then.

Clearly the Greek railway were considering converting some of their engines to burn oil, as they asked the following questions:

'1. The value in calories of coal and oil used by you.

2. The amount of fuel (coal and oil) consumed per train mile.

3. The fuel (coal and oil) consumed per ton mile.

4. The expenses for maintaining fireboxes in case of coal and oil burning.

5. The eventual saving of personnel by the use of fuel oil instead of coal (night firemen, etc) and every other useful Information thereon.'

The request was signed by S. Gialistras, General Manager.

'L11' No. 437 and at least one other 'oiler' on the scrap line at Eastleigh in late May 1951. Its days were now definitely numbered, while the poor external condition is easily explained by the more than two and half years it had spent in open store. *Jeremy Staines collection*

For whatever reason, the original letter was passed upwards to Marylebone and ended up with V.M. Barrington-Ward at the Railway Executive. It was to Marylebone that S.W. Smart, on behalf of the Southern, replied in brief terms:

'No. 1: The three (?) classes of coal used on main-line engines, 14,500 BThUs. Oil 18,750 BThUs.

No. 2: Coal – 50 lbs per mile; oil 4 gallons per mile.

No. 3: No information available.

No. 4: There is little difference apparent with recent experiences.

No. 5: There is no saving in personnel. Staff released form steam raising etc, is offset by staff employed on oil ground installations (boiler attendants etc).'

Possibly Barrington-Ward was collating replies from all four companies before responding, while even in the few words from Mr Smart we learn enough to fill another piece in the jigsaw; namely (likely some) steam raisers became boiler attendants (at Fratton at least).

With the oil-burning scheme ended, Bulleid at Brighton also replied to a request from Riddles at Marylebone as to the number of engines converted, dates of conversions and, most interestingly, miles run per type. Although some of this information has been reported previously with reference to individual the classes, it is also useful to provide a full resume.

Engine No.	Class	Date of conversion to oil burning
21C 119	WC	26-7-47
113	T9	20-9-47
114	T9	6-9-47
115	T9	30-8-47
118	T9	30-8-47
121	T9	30-8-47
148	L11	27-9-47
154	L11	4-10-47
155	L11	11-10-47
157	L11	11-10-47
170	L11	4-10-47
172	L11	37-9-47
280	T9	13-9-47
286	T9	13-9-47
303	T9	20-9-47
305	T9	18-1-47
314	T9	13-9-47
411	L11	23-8-47
437	L11	26-7-47
463	D15	25-9-47
713	T9	6-9-47

A few days (or was it a year?) later, and by now liberally daubed in contemporary graffiti, No. 437 has been moved to the rear of Eastleigh shed ready for what will be its final journey, likely Ashford. Official withdrawal was not until June 1952. Subsequent (1954) analysis of the maintenance costs of an oil burner compared with a coal-burning engine found the cost of the former to be approximately 1s per mile greater. This was described as being primarily due to the costs of firebricks but without further elaboration. *Jeremy Staines collection*

Engine No.	Class	Date of conversion to oil burning
722	T9	13-9-47
731	T9	30-8-47
740	N15	14-12-46
745	N15	4-10-47
748	N15	27-9-47
749	N15	11-10-47
752	N15	27-9-47
1625	U	6-12-47
1797	N	4-10-47
1831	N	20-9-47

Note: the above are taken from the report in the National Archives and so dates may differ slightly from information published elsewhere. We may note also that No. 34036 is not mentioned.

The class mileages run were as follows:

T9   205,284

L11   74,415

D15   20,297

WC   10,616

N15   81,725

N   21,694 *

U   63,998 *

Total: 478,031. This does not include 515S nor 34036.

*These figure do not totally correspond with that in the *Book of the...*series.

Thus almost half a million miles, some engines also working only for a matter of months before ceasing work. Whether it also meant all were actually even in service (not meant to be taken as simultaneously) or whether three were in fact permanently stored – and if so which ones – is not reported.

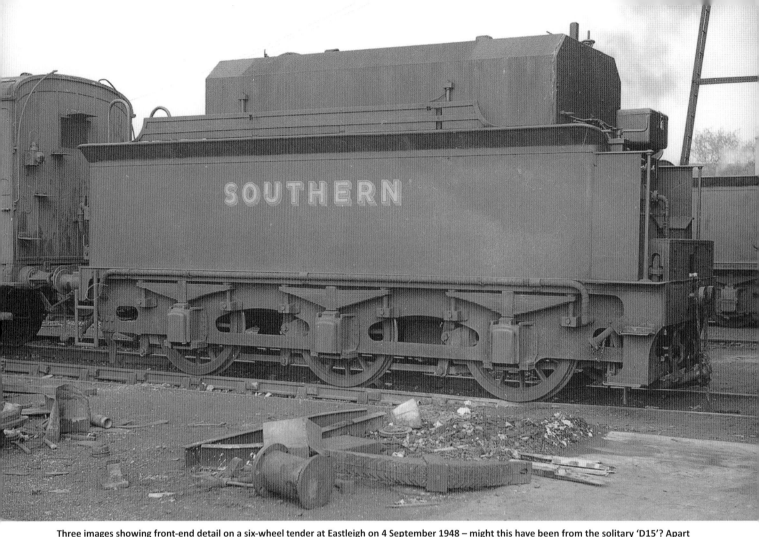

Three images showing front-end detail on a six-wheel tender at Eastleigh on 4 September 1948 – might this have been from the solitary 'D15'? Apart from the frames from one of the 'T9s' that were reused, we have no idea whether any other parts from the engines or tenders were salvaged for further use. (Oil tanks excluded.) *Mike King collection*

A former oil-burning tender believed recorded at Eastleigh and clearly no longer in use. With several of the tender tanks believed salvaged (or are the ones referred in the text as 'on the ground' meant to imply new tanks that had been delivered but were never installed), it is likely tenders with tanks still in situ may well have been seen around Eastleigh for some time post-1951. *Jeremy Staines collection*

The Cuckoo in the nest

There is more than one final twist in the oil-burning story, this time referring to No. 34036, which we recall was converted last, by which time senior management were already aware a pause had been ordered on all further installations and conversions.

It appears from what little definite information we have that it was quietly working away on the SR until the fact an oil burner was still in operation came to the attention of 'the Kremlin' – as BRB Headquarters at 222 Marylebone Road was somewhat disrespectfully referred. Questions were asked, which prompted a reply from Mr Chrimes, then the Motive Power Superintendent at Waterloo, to V.M. Barrington-Ward at BRB on 15 September 1949.

'Referring to your letter of 8 inst. Locomotive No. 34036 'West Country Class' was experimentally fitted for oil burning on the 'Laidlaw drew' system by the Chief Mechanical Engineer. [OVB, of course.]

'The engine was not so fitted until approximately October of last year when all oil burning generally was ceasing, and this engine has been working on purely experimental work in the hands of the Chief Mechanical Engineer.

'The mileage run has been very small, approximately 2,000, and no oil has been supplied by this department.

'I am now given to understand that the experiment has closed and the engine is now being reconverted for coal burning.

'It is regretted you were not advised of this at the time.'

A copy of this reply was also sent to the Chief Regional Officer.

But, now explain this. In the Irwell Press volume *The Book of the West Country and Battle of Britain Pacifics* by Richard Derry, (2008 reprint), p.109 affords details of works visits and mileages for No. 21C136/34036, with the following taken from the individual engine record card shown:

31-12-47 to 28-2-48 (BTN) 50,783 miles … 'Laidlaw Drew' oil-burning equipment.

There are then five subsequent works visits for 'D' ('Non-classified') repairs or modifications, three of these in 1948 (the first when the BR number was appended) and two in 1949. The last is shown as over two days on 3–4 March 1949. None indicate where this took place but it could have been a works or even a running shed as certainly unclassified repairs were indeed carried out at the major depots. In all cases cumulative mileages are given, which we will refer to in a moment.

Next comes a 'LC' ('Light Casual') repair, again the location is not specified but it was from 12 August to 2 September 1949. Finally another 'LC' repair from 21 October to 11 November with the note 'Converted back to coal burning'. Well the supposed start date of the trial 'approximately October last year (1948)' is clearly wrong – this should have read at least

The melancholy sight of two former oil burners breaking their journey en route to scrap, seen here at Guildford. No. 437 may be identified (ex-Eastleigh) but the second engine is not so certain. They are being shunted by a '700' class 0-6-0. With the external coupling rods still in place, which would assist in balancing as they were towed, the inside motion would almost certainly have been dismantled. It is believed both were en route for cutting at Ashford, which again begs the possibility that this might have been a way to move the one salvageable item – the tender oil tanks – to where they might be required. No oil-burning engine is believed to have ever visited Guildford in steam. *RCTS*

Speaking of scrap; this 'may' be part of the heating elements from a scrap tender. It was certainly taken on the scrap lines at the rear of Eastleigh works and also dates from the correct period. It is believed the item has been rotated through 180 degrees for ease of the cutters. In the official report of the Comptroller and Auditor General of the Civil Appropriation Accounts for the year ended 31 March 1948 published by HM Stationary Office, the Ministry of Transport spent nearly £3 million on the conversion of locomotives from coal to oil. Owing to the urgency for saving coal, work on the conversions was commenced without waiting for detailed estimates of the costs incurred. By September 1947, ninety-three locos had been or were being converted. Work was then suspended on locomotive conversion but not the storage facilities. It was estimated that 840,000 of oil was needed per annum for the full programme. In 1948 the BTC could not agree with the MoT that the scheme should be continued. The cost of operating the ninety-three converted locos was put at £279,000 pa and if completed the full programme at £3.5 million per annum. The scheme was finally abandoned in May 1948 with an estimate for converting the oil-burning engines to coal for an estimated £200 each – except for the poor Great Western, who would have to pay the reconversion costs themselves for the five engines they had initially converted and which the government used as the benchmark. Meanwhile, expenditure at an annual rate of £10,000 was being incurred on maintenance of storage depots. It is believed this continued until at least October 1949, and possibly beyond, but was subject to annual review. *S.C. Townroe*

February 1948. The end date is perhaps a bit closer, September against October 1949, and almost ties in with the response from Chrimes to Headquarters, even it did take almost five weeks from Chrimes' reply for the engine to enter shops. To be fair, it may even have been out of use during this period. But what cannot be challenged is the mileage. At the time of being converted back to coal the recorded mileage was 65,827. Subtract the starting mileage when she was converted to oil (50,783) and we have mileage run in oil burning condition as 15,044. 'very small, approximately 2,000' *Really!* From April 1948, and so for most of the period in operation as an oil burner, No. 34036 was based at Eastleigh.

So do we smell a rat, despite the fact that on the face of it, it is a perfectly reasonable explanation from Chrimes. Well if there is rat it has to be in the spectre of 'Leader' 36001 again. In 1948 and 1949, Bulleid was still using what had once been his full autonomy, although now, of course, he really should

have sought permission from BRB Headquarters. 'Leader' was proceeding with the knowledge and consent of BRB and we know Bulleid had intended it to burn oil. With the engine getting closed to completion, was this the trial to test if this type of burner was suitable? Supposition maybe and with absolutely no supporting evidence, but coincidence yes and, in the opinion of the present writer, too strong a coincidence to ignore. Chrimes was innocent; he asked for information and could only report what he was imparted. We may even wonder where the necessary oil was obtained from and how No. 34036 was fuelled, although a report of 22/23 November 1948 comments that 6,000 gallons of oil remained at Eastleigh (we hate being contradictory again but elsewhere in the same memo a second figure of 10,000 gallons is mentioned. Surely too this must have been in tank cars and not the fixed storage tanks? And if the former, we can imagine the Petroleum board shouting rather loudly for their tank cars to be returned!)

After its time at Fratton and subsequent withdrawal at the end of 1951, No. 701S, the former SR No. 2284, found its way to Brighton, where it was recorded in 1951 no doubt awaiting scrap. *Tony Sedgwick/Ian Wilkins*

Perhaps if the true mileage had come out, and with it the true purpose, this was why Bulleid seems to give up without a fight; that is until now for we are 99.9 per cent certain no one has previously tied up the connection between the correspondence and engine record card and ongoing developments at Brighton. Finally, we might ask how long No. 34036 might have continued working if no one had spotted it – presumably she was kept well away from the Waterloo at the very least!

We move now to the question of what to do with the assets, which involved both locomotives and depot facilities.

The paper trail on this appears to commence on 11 January 1950 with a note from Mr Chrimes and again to Barrington-Ward. It was headed 'Abandonment of coal/oil conversion scheme and disposal of equipment'.

At this time the suggestion for Fratton was that the installation be leased to a private firm as a going concern (for what purpose?) with no objection raised by the Mechanical and Electrical Engineer or the Motive Power Departments. Eastleigh was still stated to be under consideration, while at Exmouth Junction Motive Power could see no further use for the installation and its position within the site made any potential outside use impractical.

Things get more interesting so far as Eastleigh is concerned, with a note again from Chrimes to the same recipient on 27 June (but referring back to an earlier letter of 10 May, which has not been located). This time we are advised the M & EE has 'signified his agreement' to utilise one of the redundant

buildings as a repair shop for diesel and electric locomotives. We are informed that eight (out of eleven for the whole of Southern Region) diesel-electric shunting locomotives are in the 1950 programme for allocation to Eastleigh for operation in the Eastleigh, Southampton and Bournemouth areas with consideration of suitable facilities for maintenance at Eastleigh.

The report goes on to give some very useful information on the buildings at Eastleigh, thus, 'the redundant coal/oil conversion buildings were inspected. The larger building situated some 500ft east of the Running Shed is brick built with corrugated asbestos roof and divided into two sections by a brick partition. One section contains two boilers and the other steam driver fuel pumps. The flooring is of concrete. This building appears to be eminently suitable for conversion into a Maintenance Shop for diesel-electric shunting engines. It is estimated that it could accommodate two locomotives at a time on one road and also allow for a workshop and stores space. The main alterations requires consist of the removal of the existing boilers and pumping plant, the provision of an entrance for the locomotives in the end wall of the boiler section and a further opening in the partition wall to allow the work to extend into the other section. It would also be necessary to extend the roof into this building. There is already a siding in existence running alongside the building which is not used and this could be realigned to provide the necessary access to the sheds. The site of the proposed fuelling plant for shunting locomotives is adjacent to the building but would need to be moved a short distance to allow room for the access roads.

The buildings of the former boiler and pump house at Fratton remained standing until the end of steam. The concrete supports for the oil tanks are also visible in this view from 8 August 1965 showing No. 76033 alongside. Almost certainly the last remnants of oil firing from this period in time survive not on the Southern, but instead on the Western where the same type of concrete supports for long removed oil storage tanks may still be seen at the Didcot Railway Centre in 2020. *Tony Harris*

'The second building is situated just outside the east end of the main running shed but is only about half the size and is therefore not considered to be large enough for the purpose required. No use could therefore be made of this building. I recommend that the larger building be acquired for conversion into a Maintenance shop and shall be glad if you advise me if this can be agreed. Upon approval it will be necessary for a scheme to be prepared in conjunction with the Chief Civil Engineer for the necessary alterations. As a suitable Maintenance building will be required early in 1951, I shall be glad to know as soon as possible if you agree to this proposal.'

From correspondence dating from the following year 1951, we know from subsequent (part) correspondence that approval for plans and estimates was given in 1950 but added to which was a second reference to what in effect was a 'Plan B'. This now refers to, 'The small building at Eastleigh housing two boilers for steaming purposes could be used for the storage of heavy material, accommodation for which is at present in a dilapidated condition. However, before doing so the two boilers would have to be removed.'

Yet again more questions than answers. Which small building, and similarly was the heavy material mentioned related to the diesel shunter maintenance?

Fratton was again mentioned – clearly the private use previously mentioned had not gone ahead – with the two sections; boiler house and engine and pump house. Again there was mention that these contained material (boilers/pumps) awaiting disposal. It was suggested the structure as a whole might be used for office accommodation and an ambulance classroom.

Fortunately this report at last also gives us useful information on the ground facilities at Exmouth Junction. 'Only one building was erected at Exmouth Junction, this is not within the precincts of the Motive Power Depot but is actually situated between the depot and the Carriage and Wagon Repair Shop on the north side of the Exmouth Junction Goods Yard shunting neck. The building

The rear of Eastleigh shed – please try and ignore the Adams 'Radial' and 'E6/B4' tank engines. The point of the views is again the building behind, with evidence pointing towards this having been one of the boiler houses. *Roger Thornton/M. Stribens*

is divided into two sections, one housing the pump and machinery and the other three locomotive-type boilers. A portion of the boiler room has been partitioned off and is at present being used by the Carriage & Wagon Examiner as a Barrow repair Shop. As access to the building from the Motive power depot could only be gained by crossing a busy shunting neck, I do not consider this building by this department for any purpose.'

(We should add that the same memo also referred to former oil facilities at Bath. This information has been added to the Appendix.)

There appears to be nothing else reported until 1952, when Mr H.H. Swift, then the Mechanical and Electrical Engineer for the Southern region based at Brighton, refers to the disposal of equipment from the scheme. Various sundry items including pipes, flanges and valves are referred to, as well as six tender fuel tanks that Mr Swift confirms have been allocated to the diesel locomotive fuelling stations at Eastleigh and Hither Green. It had been hoped that some of the redundant material might have found a use in fuelling the cross-Channel steamers at Folkestone and Dover but it appears much was subsequently discovered not to be of use.

The following year, on 20 January and then again on 25 February 1953, we are told that thirteen tender fuel tanks 'lying on the ground at Eastleigh' have been earmarked for schemes already authorised or under consideration, 'as reported in my letter of 28 October last ...' (not located).

In addition, there were two tanks mounted on old tender frames being used to provide storage accommodation for heavy fuel oil being used at Eastleigh Works. Mr Swift then asks, 'at what price they could be transferred to this region?' This must mean the two former LNER/LMS often recorded around this time. He concludes, 'The remaining tanks at Eastleigh and the one at Ashford will not be required for railway purposes.'

With the smaller engines from the Southern scrapped, again the reader might be forgiven for thinking this might be the end – but again not and instead we move forward to the start of August 1954 with a note from a Mr Pope at BRB to Mr Reep Lintern at the Ministry of Transport and Civil Aviation, as it was then known. Almost out of the blue, Mr Pope refers to the BRB 'getting out some facts and figures of employing oil for firing steam locomotives on the Western Region and on the stretch of line between Perth, Inverness and Wick where only one class of locomotive only as a general rule is employed'. A report and correspondence was subsequently produced and forwarded at the end of the same month.

This interesting paperwork contains figures on the 1947 conversions as well as an analysis based on what point the price of oil becomes economic for firing steam locomotives.

In summary terms, the costs in 1947 refer to the cost of converting 1,229 locomotives as well as the depot installations as £3,600,000.

This resulted in a reduction in coal consumption of 1,040,000 tons replaced by oil consumption of 832,000.

In order to break even, the cost of oil must not be more than 84/- per ton.

The paperwork then goes on to describe the theoretical conversions/operational costs of converting either 107 or 184 locomotives but without mentioning where this was being considered for. So far as specific detail is concerned, there is no more talk of the WR and instead the three motive power depots at Perth, Inverness and Wick are mentioned.

Allowing for inflation between January 1947 and August 1954, the 1947 cost of the locomotive conversions stated as having been £1,065,000 had now risen to £1,886,000. There was a similar increase in the figure for the proposed depot installations.

Nothing though came of the scheme – although a single pannier tank was converted at Swindon to burn oil around 1956 it is believed to have been simply a means of using up existing stocks.

Other than that the remaining paperwork goes on to describe tests with shunting engines burning coke on the Midland and Eastern regions, both of which resulted in abject failure. It then explains in great detail how the steam locomotive in general terms was outdated and outmoded when compared with the efficiency of the diesel so far as efficiency in burning fuel was concerned. We need not dwell further on history already known.

This then really is the end of the story of the Southern Railways 'obligation' to convert a proportion of its engines to burn oil. Successful in some ways, but it seems mainly from the point of view of the workload – if not the cleanliness of the crews – and certainly successful with the ability to almost produce steam on demand. It could be considered unsuccessful because if the burner and flow of oil were not 'in sync', then the resulting outpourings from the chimney must have most unpleasant for all concerned. It would also mean a perhaps shorter life for some of the various 4-4-0s than might otherwise have been expected, for as we know when the burner finally went out for the final time they would never steam again.

Similarly, we will now never know how if an 'H15', or a 'Merchant Navy', had been considered and converted it might have performed.

Oil firing may have officially ceased on the nationalised Britain's Railways in 1948 but it was not quite the end for BR later converted the solitary LNER Garratt to burn oil, while Swindon also converted 57xx 0-6-0PT No. 3711 to burn oil between 1958 and 1959. In the latter case it was intended that the engine would use up any remaining supplies at old Oak Common. We should also not forget that the Gas Turbine 18000 (not 18100) also ran on heavy oil and was operational between 1950 and 1960.

The ramifications of 1946–51 would also continue to reverberate among those in charge of making decisions on motive power for some years to come, and not just with the paper exercise re Scotland and the Western Region mentioned previously.

Messrs Johnson and Long in their book *British Railways Engineering 1948–80* (MEP Publications 1981) comment, 'When the memory of this wasted investment in the use of oil for traction was so fresh in the minds of railway engineers, it

DS680 at Eastleigh on 3 March 1963, but look behind and then to the right. We have the diesel depot behind *and* to the right the end of the former boiler/pump house; proof the former did not occupy the site of the latter. It is believed the boiler/pump house here was demolished soon after. (It is pure coincidence that No. DS680 bears the allocation 'Lancing Works'.) *Tony Molyneaux*

was understandable that there was some concern at the prospect of diesel traction on a large scale.'

They continue that Riddles decision to continue with steam was based on three factors: 'Firstly investment resources available to British Railways were severely limited. Secondly it was possible to buy about five steam units for one diesel of equivalent power. And finally, oil supplies were subject to strategic and foreign currency objections – [fluctuations might be a better word] as had been so evident in 1948.'

The railways should be seen as coming out of the whole episode with their heads held high. It is the government and all its associates who need to take responsibility, not just for asking what was just not possible but more so for having realised very early on the whole was unsustainable and then allowing it to continue.

Appendix 1
Bath Locomotive Depot

The following is a copy of a memorandum located within the SR oil burning-related files at the National Archives. While specifically relating to Bath, it is of particular interest as the Somerset and Dorset line from Bath was a joint line between the LMS and SR.

'PART I – FOR SPECIAL CONSIDERATION R.E.C,

7,463. Conversion of locomotives to oil fuel.

Read R.E.C. minute 9,821 referring to Operating: Committee (in connection with M.&E. Com.Min.2,931) suggestion that one locomotive shed (e.g. Bath LMS) be completely converted so that economic effect of conversion to oil burning may be more accurately assessed.

REPORT. The following locomotives are allocated to Bath (L.M.S.) Motive Power Depot:

Class 5 mixed-traffic tender	5*
Class 7 S.&D. 2-8-0 freight tender	11*
Class 4 freight tender	12*
Class 2 passenger tank	4
Class1 passenger tank	3
Class 3 freight tender	1
Total	36

In connection with the conversion of locomotives from coal to oil burning, it has already been agreed that the 28 locomotives marked with an asterisk should be converted to oil burning, leaving 8 coal-burning locomotives allocated to Bath depot. In order to reduce the number of classes of locomotives, arrangements could be made for the 1 class 3 freight tender locomotive to be replaced by a class 4 freight tender locomotive,

making 13 class 4 freight tender locomotives but it is understood the L.M.S. Chief Mechanical Engineer would have difficulty in converting the 4 class 2 passenger tender and the 3 class 1 passenger tank locomotives to oil burning, particularly as additional drawing office work would be involved.

If this could be overcome, it would be an advantage in this particular instance for all locomotives allocated to Bath (L.M.S.) Motive Power Depot to be converted to oil burning during the period oil is being burned in British locomotives, as this particular Depot requires modernisation; the coal stage is condemned and will have to be replaced by a coaling plant which will necessitate a reconstructed layout in an already congested yard.

Owing to physical conditions, there is no room for expansion of the yard, and it would be an advantage, when modernisation is being carried out, to avoid having to deal with loaded and empty coal wagons and ash wagons, and to confine the work of fuelling locomotives to oil.

As mentioned in the final chapter, disposal of assets was mentioned in a memorandum from Waterloo dated 26 September 1951. The following was the reference to Bath:

'The installation at bath consists of one brick building in good condition which at present houses sundry material awaiting disposal. It is considered that the building could be converted into a Driver's lobby with accommodation for lockers on the ground floor and the upper portion utilised for office accommodation. The existing Driver's lobby is very small with little room for Notice' etc. and a locker room does not exist. The present office accommodation is also in a bad state of repair.'

'S&D' 2-8-0 at Bath Green Park. The concept of turning a complete depot over to burn oil was in many ways perfectly logical, although it is likely with the locomotives available and their related duties, 'topping-up' facilities would likely have been needed at Templecombe and possible Branksome. But what does not make any sense whatsoever is how the authorities seem to fail to mention the conditions that would have existed on the footplate of a 2-8-0 (or other engine) pounding through Combe Down Tunnel. We know from Peter Smith (*see* bibliography) that conditions were poor on the ascent out of Bath, with at least one crew overcome by fumes in the confined quarters of the tunnel; what it might have been like with an oil burner hardly bears considering. (A view of an S&D 2-8-0 by the late Ivo Peters with the two redundant oil tanks behind the engine appears as Image No. 3 in *Somerset & Dorset in the 'Fifties Part 1 1950–1954*, published by OPC.) *Transport Treasury*

Appendix 2
The oil-burning locomotive

As mentioned on a number of occasions within the text, we have been unable to locate any formal instructions as to the operation of the converted engines.

There is, however, available to us the pamphlet *Oil-Burning Locomotive, The 'Inside' Story for Enthusiasts,* by R.J .Eaton (Transportation Press, undated, but c.1947). Ninety-nine per cent of this refers to the GWR conversions but operation of the converted engines on the other railway was no doubt almost identical, and in consequence the relevant sections are reproduced here:

'The man who once asked, "Which comes first the chicken or the egg," might well ask about the oil-burning locomotive: "Which comes first the oil or the steam?"

'No steam, no flowing oil. No flowing oil, no flame. No flame, no steam. We could keep going around in circles.

'How, then is lighting up accomplished?

'The key to the answer is a connection under the frame, just behind one of the rear driving wheels, to which is coupled a steam supply pipe from another engine in steam or in the sheds, from one of the boiler-washing steam lines. The boiler steam supply valve on the steam fountain is closed and the auxiliary steam valve (on the manifold) opened.

'After the auxiliary steam has been admitted, the appropriate valve is opened to allow steam to pass to the steam heater manifold on the tender. The oil tank heater system is then turned on fully until, after a period of time depending upon the weather conditions prevailing, the oil reaches a temperature of about 150 degrees F.

'The burner cleaner having been used for a while, and the fuel regulator tested to ensure that it has its full operating range (it works around a quadrant), there is preparation for lighting up.

'This can be done after the temperature has registered 100 degrees F. The tender oil supply cock is turned on and the oil strainer "worked".

'After the dampers have been half opened, actual lighting-up is carried out by placing lighted oily-waste (usually in a long-handled) wire cage poked through the firebox door peep-hole) under the oil burner. Then the fuel regulator is turned on slightly until the oil ignites, when the burner stream is turned on.

'The auxiliary blower is next turned on and the oil and steam supplies adjusted so as to give a smokeless flame.

'When the firebox has been sufficiently heated and 50 lbs pressure reached on the gauge, the boiler steam is admitted to the manifold and at 70 lbs the auxiliary steam supply is turned off.

'Lighting up from cold is a gradual process taking three hours or more.

'Closing down is not such a lengthy operation. First the tender oil cock is shut. When the flame goes out the fuel regulator is closed. Finally all valves and dampers and the steam supply from fountain to manifold are 'shut down'.

'A wise precaution against fire, either during lighting up or while the engine is in service, is the provision of fire extinguishers and syringes on both sides of the locomotive. These appliances are fitted on the exterior lower mounting step, well away from the controls, and so are available to the crew even if it should be necessary to "abandon ship".'

The same publication gave details of 'The Fireman's new job':

'As the change of equipment on an oil-burning locomotive is entirely due to change of fuel, the fireman particularly has a new kind of job to do. Instead of shovelling chunks of coal from tender to firehole, he sits and turns valve controls. This new way of firing requires no less vigilance than coaling. Indeed, the fireman must keep a sharp eye on the driver's actions, noting the position of the regulator from time to time and adjusting the fire to steam requirements.

'The four principal duties of the fireman are:

1. To adjust the heaters in the oil tank so as to maintain the correct temperature. (He must keep an eye on the thermometer.)

2. To control the flow of oil to the burner.

3. To regulate the passage of steam to the atomiser.

4. To ensure that the correct amount of air is let into the firebox by opening and closing the damper doors in the ashpan.

'A fifth job is the cleaning of the burner jet by applying a steam blast through the burner cleaner provided.

'All the fuel and burner controls are necessarily on the fireman's side of the cab, and an extra gauge, showing the burner steam pressure, is in front of him.

'Then below the five steam supply valves, and within handy range, is the horizontal wheel that regulates the flow of fuel. The fireman operates this wheel almost continuously and also, not so frequently, a wheel at his right. This second wheel controls the dampers and ensures that the right amount of air is admitted to the firebox.

'As the locomotive runs he watches the top of the chimney and by careful manipulation of the valves and

An almost 'what might have been'. 'T9' No. 731 freshly converted and in clean condition at Eastleigh in 1947. Post-1951 it was not quite the end for oil burning on BR as the unique ex LNER Beyer-Garrett 2-8-0 + 0-8-2 No. 69999 was so equipped in the early 1950s, while on the WR a pannier tank was also equipped to burn oil (as well as No. 18000 mentioned in the text.)

dampers, ensures that the fuel burns from a clean burner so as to give nothing but a brownish haze over the chimney.

'During darkness his guide to correct combustion is the colour of the flame that can be seen through the peephole in the firebox door.

'In addition to operating the fuel and flame, the fireman does other jobs, just as he would on a coal-burning engine, such as tending the injectors and, perhaps, the sanding gear.'

Appendix 3
The known plans

The following is a list of the plans known to have once existed dealing with oil burning from the perspective of the Chief Civil Engineer's department – there may, of course, have been others! It also indicated how rapidly the CCE's department progressed with the work while sometimes also affording useful details not reported elsewhere.

Date	Plan No.	Series No.	Location	Detail
	2994D		Fratton	Oil fuel installation
25-10-46	2590G	9	Fratton	Foundations for fuel oil storage tanks
28-10-46	2590G	10	Fratton	Plan and sections, oil pipes
28-10-46	2590G	11	Fratton	Pump house oil pipes, plan and section
31-10-46	2590G	12	Fratton	Foundations for fuel oil storage tanks
16-11-46	2590G	13	Fratton	Drainage plan
26-11-46	2994B	2	Fratton	Oil fuelling of locos setting out plan *
26-11-46	2994B	3	Fratton	Foundations of boiler house
26-11-46	2994B	4	Fratton	Boiler house
26-11-46	2994B	5	Fratton	Pump house
26-11-46	2994B	6	Fratton	Walkways in pump house
26-11-46	2994B	7	Fratton	Steelwork details
26-11-46	2994B	8	Fratton	R C raft details
26-11-46	2994B	9	Fratton	R C culvert for oil pipes
26-11-46	2994B	10	Fratton	R C culvert for steam pipes
26-11-46	2994B	11	Fratton	Walkways and staircase for storage tanks
26-11-46	2994B	12	Fratton	Ditto No. 11
26-11-46	2994B	13	Fratton	Filling arms supports
26-11-46	2994B	14	Fratton	Hose racks
26-11-46	2994B	15	Fratton	Access roadway plan – cross section
28-11-46	2994B	16	Fratton	Details of site storage tanks
2-12-46	2994B	17	Fratton	Amended plan and section – oil pipes
2-12-46	2994B	18	Fratton	Details of smokebox ducts and chimney Sheet 1
2-12-46	2994B	19	Fratton	Ditto Sheet 2
2-12-46	2994B	20	Fratton	Pump house oil pipes – amended
2-12-46	2994B	21	Fratton	Steam pipes arrangement
6-12-46	2994B	22	Fratton	Section through steam pipe culvert shewing new steps to engine pit
16-12-46	2994B	23	Fratton	Revised drainage plan
30-12-46	2994B	24	Fratton	General arrangement of civil engineering work
20-1-47	2994B	25	Fratton	Pump house oil pipes – revised
31-1-47	2994B	26	Fratton	Details of reinforced raft – amended
31-1-47	2994B	27	Fratton	R C culvert for oil pipe amended
31-1-47	2994B	28	Fratton	R C culvert for steam pipe amended
31-1-47	2994B	29	Fratton	Concrete access road amended plan and cross section
31-1-47	2994B	30	Fratton	Revised drainage plan
31-1-47	2994B	31	Fratton	General arrangement of civil engineering works amended
3-2-47	2994B	32	Fratton	Steel for pump house boilers spacing of purlins
7-2-47	2994B	33	Fratton	Further amended details of reinforced raft
7-2-47	2994B	34	Fratton	Further amended details R C culvert for oil pipe
7-2-47	2994B	35	Fratton	Further amended details R C culvert for steam pipe

Date	Plan No.	Series No.	Location	Detail
7-2-47	2994B	36	Fratton	Further amended details revised drainage plan
24-2-47	2994B	37	Fratton	Details of chimney, boiler house
24-2-47	2994B	38	Fratton	Details of chimney weathering, water storage tank and supports.
24-2-47	2994B	39	Fratton	Details of dampers, boiler house
1-3-47	2994B	40	Fratton	Boiler house revised floor details
13-3-47	2994B	51		General arrangement of oil fuel installation
25-3-47	2994B	53		General arrangement of civil engineering works
1-4-47	2994B	54	Fratton	Diagrammatic layout of boiler pits and walls
9-4-47	2994B	55	Fratton	Boiler foundations
16-5-47	2994B	56	Fratton	Boiler house flues revised detail of duct to fan inlet
23-5-47	2994B	57	Fratton	Steelwork for boiler and pump houses
23-9-47	2994B	58	Fratton	Details and arrangements of boiler house further revised drawing
13-11-47	2994B	60	Fratton	Oil fuel installation drainage modifications
27-2-48	2994B	63	Fratton	Conversion of locos to oil, fuel fire extinguisher boxes
17-11-50	2247 K/W	5	Eastleigh	Proposed diesel loco maintenance shed
5-1-51	2247 K/W	9	Eastleigh	Fuelling station for diesel shunting locos
4-4-51	2247 K/W	10	Eastleigh	MPD Proposed maintenance shop for diesel locos
Aug 46	44607		Eastleigh	Loco. Proposed oil fuel installation
Sept. 46	44645		Eastleigh	Loco. Proposed diagram of oil pipes
Oct. 46	44720		Eastleigh	Loco. Proposed circular oil tanks
Oct. 46	44737		Eastleigh	Loco. Proposed installation
Oct. 46	44788		Eastleigh	Circular fuel tanks foundations
Oct. 46	44976		Eastleigh	Ditto
Oct. 46	45973		Eastleigh	Oil fuel installation plan
Dec. 46	45263		Eastleigh	MPD alterations to tracks to suit location of No. 2 boiler house
Dec. 46	45271		Eastleigh	MPD conversion of locos steam pipe outlets
Dec. 46	5905		Eastleigh	Details of pipe bridge
Dec. 46	45334		Eastleigh	MPD oil pipe arrangements
Dec. 46	45393		Eastleigh	MPD pump house oil pipes
Dec. 46	45396		Eastleigh	MPD fabricated steam pipes
Dec. 46	45397		Eastleigh	MPD steam pipe arrangement
Jan. 47	45339		Eastleigh	MPD engine shed pipes for steaming locos
Jan. 47	45375		Eastleigh	MPD general arrangement of civil engineering work
Jan. 47	45376		Eastleigh	MPD tank foundations
Jan. 47	54377		Eastleigh	MPD RC rafts tracks north of pump house
Jan. 47	45378		Eastleigh	MPD RC rafts tracks south of pump house
Jan. 47	45379		Eastleigh	MPD RC rafts pump house
Jan. 47	45380		Eastleigh	MPD walkways to pump house
Jan. 47	45381		Eastleigh	MPD arrangement of boiler house No. 1
Jan. 47	45382		Eastleigh	MPD floor details boiler house No. 1
Jan. 47	45383		Eastleigh	MPD arrangement of boiler house No. 2 **
Jan. 47	45384		Eastleigh	MPD floor details boiler house No. 2 **
Jan. 47	45385		Eastleigh	MPD steel for boiler and pump house
Jan. 47	45386		Eastleigh	MPD oil fuel layout of boiler house flues
Jan. 47	45387		Eastleigh	MPD oil fuel details of smokeboxes, ducts and chimneys
Jan. 47	45668		Eastleigh	MPD details of connections to storage tanks
Feb. 47	45574		Eastleigh	Boiler house No. 1 floor details
Feb. 47	45977		Eastleigh	Details of tank foundations
Feb. 47	45577		Eastleigh	Pump house walkways sheet 2

Date	Plan No.	Series No.	Location	Detail
Feb. 47	45578		Eastleigh	Steelwork for boiler and pump houses
Mar. 47	45753		Eastleigh	Connections to storage tanks
Mar. 47	45668		Fratton	Oil fuel: diagrammatic layout boiler pits
Mar. 47	45773		E/Junction	Insulating storage tanks
Mar. 47	45762		E or EJ?	Boiler house No. 1 boiler foundations
Apr. 47	45810		E or EJ?	Steelwork for pump house
Apr. 47	45811		E or EJ?	Boiler house No. 1 constructional detail
Apr. 47	45812		E or EJ?	Boiler house No. 2 floor details
Apr. 47	45843		E or EJ?	Boiler house No. 2 details of steam pipes
May. 47	45845		Eastleigh	Boiler house and pump house details of steam pipes
May. 47	46553		Eastleigh	General arrangement of civil engineering work
May. 47	45905		Eastleigh	General arrangement of pipe bridge
May. 47	45906		Eastleigh	General arrangement of pump house
May. 47	45907		Eastleigh	Steel for boiler and pump houses
May. 47	45908		Eastleigh	Ditto
May. 47	45909		Eastleigh	Boiler house No. 1 boiler foundation
May. 47	45910		Eastleigh	Boiler and pump house revised roof arrangements
May. 47	45911		Eastleigh	Boiler house No. 1 floor details
May. 47	45912		Eastleigh	Boiler house No. 1 arrangement and details
May. 47	45913		Eastleigh	Rafts under track, steps and ramp
May. 47	46944		Eastleigh	Boiler house No. 2 floor details
May. 47	45945		Eastleigh	Boiler house arrangement and details
May. 47	45946		Eastleigh	Track supports, steel doors, chimney weathering for boiler houses 1 and 2
Jan. 48	46823		Eastleigh	Boiler house No. 2 boiler pits and smokeboxes
Mar. 47	46107		Eastleigh	Boiler house No. 1 flues etc. Sheet 1
Mar. 47	45969		Eastleigh	Boiler house Nos 1 & 2 chimney details. Sheet 2
Mar. 47	45962		Eastleigh	Water tank weathering. Sheet 3
Mar. 47	46108		Eastleigh	Boiler house No. 2 flues etc. Sheet 4
Jun. 47	46118		Eastleigh	Cross section of pit, boiler house No. 1
Jun. 47	45995		Eastleigh	Revised details of tank foundations
Jul. 47	46088		Eastleigh	Pump house roof purlin spacing on eaves slope
Oct. 47	46335		Eastleigh	Oil fuel: arrangement for unloading road fuel vehicles
Oct. 47	46443		Eastleigh	Oil fuel: proposed tidiness scheme
Sep. 48	49878		Eastleigh	Proposed fuelling station for diesel locos
16-8-46	2250 J/S	3	Eastleigh	Proposed oil fuel installation
6-9-46	2250 J/S	4	Eastleigh	Ditto
19-9-46	2250 J/S	5	Eastleigh	Ditto with unloading headed shewn
23-10-46	2250 J/S	7	Eastleigh	Proposed oil fuel installation
4-11-46	2250 J/S	8	Eastleigh	Ditto amended
5-12-46	2250 J/S	10	Eastleigh	Plan of alterations to track to sui location of No. 2 boiler house
6-12-46	2250 J/S	11	Eastleigh	Proposed oil fuel installation
18-3-47	2250 J/S	12	Eastleigh	Oil fuel installation amended site plan
6-11-47	2250 J/S	14	Eastleigh	Oil fuel depot proposed tidiness
5-10-48	2250 J/S	23	Eastleigh	Fuelling station for diesel shunting locos

* This plan only marked as 'Cancelled'.

** The terms 'Boiler House No. 1' and 'Boiler House No. 2' are not explained. (Unless in the records a form of shorthand has been used and which in reality could perhaps mean 'Boiler House, No. 1 boiler, No. 2 boiler.')

We should also not ignore the fact that the separate CME's drawing office would have prepared drawings applicable to the locomotive and tender conversions. These would be the subject of a separate register.

Appendix 4
Sample engine record cards

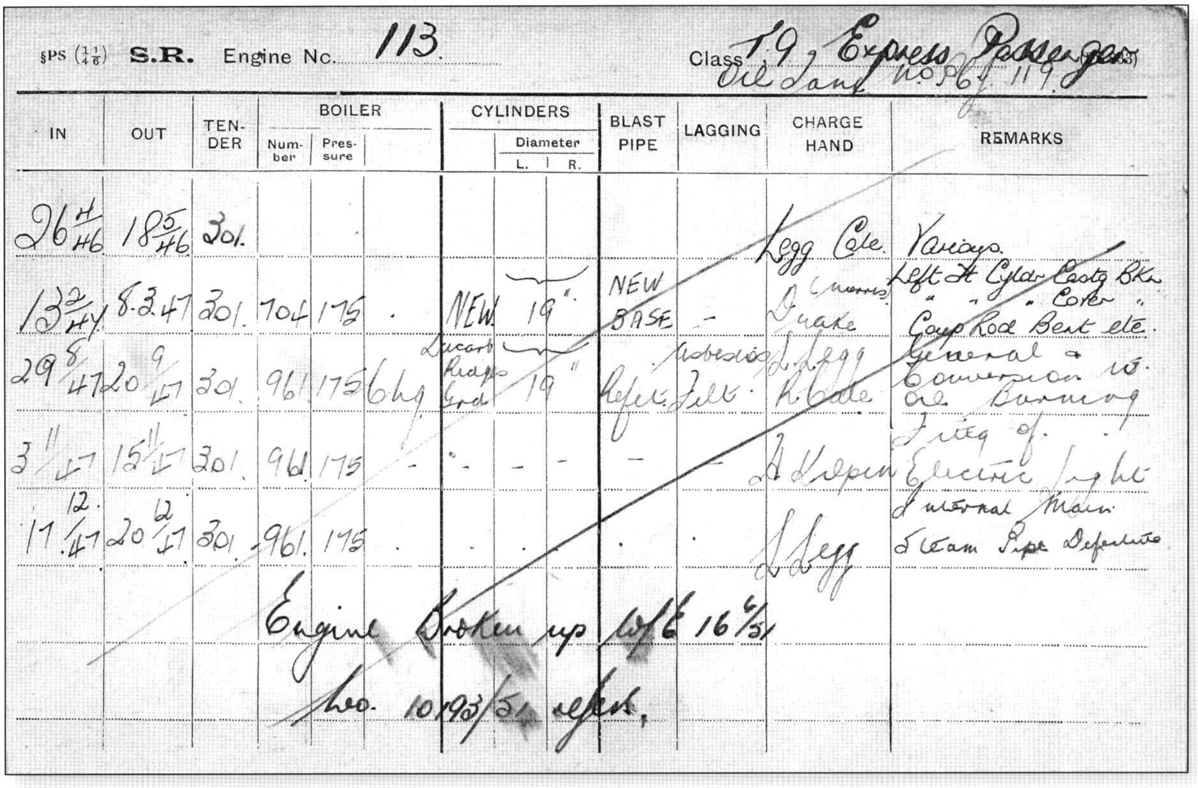

§PS (11/48) **S.R.** Engine No. 113. Class T.9 Express Passenger (D.3)
Oil Tank No. P67 119.

IN	OUT	TEN-DER	BOILER Number	BOILER Pressure		CYLINDERS	Diameter L.	Diameter R.	BLAST PIPE	LAGGING	CHARGE HAND	REMARKS
26/4/46	18/5/46	301.									Legg Cole.	Various.
13/2/47	8.3.47	301.	704	175	.	NEW	19"		NEW BASE	-	Drake (Morris)	Left H Cylr Castg Bkn / " " Cover " / Coup Rod Bent etc.
29/8/47	20/9/47	301.	961	175	6hg	Ducarb Rings Grd	19"		Refit.	Asbestos Fill.	L Legg R Cole	General & Conversion to Oil Burning
3/11/47	15/11/47	301.	961	175	-	-	-	-	-	-	A Kemp	Fitting of Electric Light
17/12/47	20/12/47	301.	961.	175	.	.	.	.	.	.	L Legg	Internal Main Steam Pipe Defective

Engine Broken up W/E 16/6/51
Wo. 10193/51 refers.

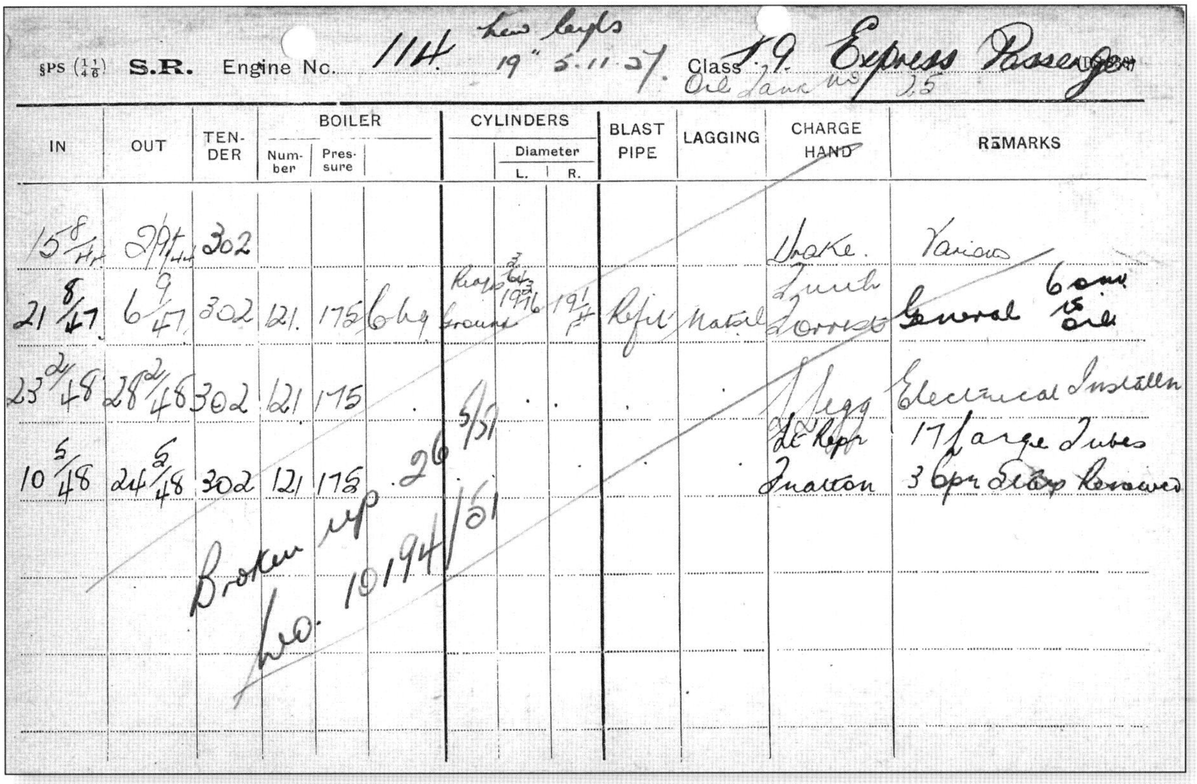

§PS (11/48) **S.R.** Engine No. 114. New Cyls 19" 5.11.37. Class T.9 Express Passenger (D.3)
Oil Tank No 25

IN	OUT	TEN-DER	BOILER Number	BOILER Pressure		CYLINDERS	Diameter L.	Diameter R.	BLAST PIPE	LAGGING	CHARGE HAND	REMARKS
15/8/44	29/9/44	302									Drake.	Various
21/8/47	6/9/47	302	121.	175	6hg	Rings Ground	19 3/4 1936	19 1/4	Refit	Natal	Smith Morris	General 6 Conv to Oil
23/2/48	28/2/48	302	121	175	.	.	.	.	.	.	L Legg	Electrical Installn
10/5/48	24/5/48	302	121	175	.	.	.	.	.	.	Le Kemp Tnatton	17 Large Tubes 36 pr Stays Renewed

Broken up 26/5/51
Wo. 10194/51

30115

§PS (1 1/4 6) **S.R.** Engine No. (115) two cyls. 12&27 19" Class T.9 Express Passenger
Oil tank as 2/34 1/2

IN	OUT	TEN-DER	BOILER			CYLINDERS		BLAST PIPE	LAGGING	CHARGE HAND	REMARKS
			Number	Pressure		Diameter L. R.					
17/6/46	29/6/46	303	119	175	Chg.	Re Bored	19¾"	Refit		Packard Cole.	General
19/8/47	30/8/47	303	119	175	-			new cap. 19/5/51	-	Legg	Conversion to Oil burning
18/12/47	29/12/47	303	119	175	.	.	.			Legg	Electrical Installation
19/5/48	5/6/48	303	301	175	Chg	Re Bored Top	up	Refit Natdl		Smith	Tubes. Box Tube Plate. Stays Ferrules
						Engine Broken up 10/9/5/51					

§PS (1 1/4 6) **S.R.** Engine No. 118 two cyls 19·9·6·28 Class T.9 Express Passenger
Oil tank as 2042/2/5

IN	OUT	TEN-DER	BOILER			CYLINDERS		BLAST PIPE	LAGGING	CHARGE HAND	REMARKS
			Number	Pressure		Diameter L. R.					
23/4/46	1/9/46	306	302	175	Chg		19½"	Refit	Natdl	Drake Forest.	General
19/8/47	30/8/47	306	302	175	-	- -	cap. new	-	Legg	Conversion to Oil burning
13/2/48	21/2/48	306	302	175	.	26/7/51	.		Legg	Electrical Installation
					Broken up two 10/96/51					

34036

§PS (1 1/4 6) **S.R.** Engine No. (21C 136.) Class 1C (PS 833)

IN	OUT	TENDER	BOILER Number	Pressure		CYLINDERS Diameter L.	R.	BLAST PIPE	LAGGING	CHARGE HAND	REMARKS
17/2/47	8.3.47	3281	1296	280		L.Hd 18" NEW		-	Fibre Glass	Roberts Cole	Left Cylinder Cast fractured. Bogie
31/6/47	20/2/48	3281	1296	280	Lifted	Cracks Removed Refit		-	Lt Reps	Brighton	Pistons Glands & Boxes Guides Wheels
11/5/48	22/5/48	3281	1296	28		Reft	-		Glass Fibre	H. Kilpin	Oil Burning Equip
10/8/48	21/8/48	3281	1296	280					Fibre Glass	L Legg	
7/9/48	11/9/48	3281	1296	280					Fibre Glass	L. Legg	alterations
8/2/49	19/2/49	3281	1296	280					Fibre Glass	G Kilpin	apparatus
3/3/49	5/3/49	3281	1296	280						G Kilpin	

§PS (5 80) **B.R. (S.)** Engine No. 34036 Class WC (PS 833)

IN	OUT	TENDER	BOILER Number	Pressure		CYLINDERS Diameter L.	R.	BLAST PIPE	LAGGING	CHARGE HAND	REMARKS
30/3/54	3/4/54	3281	12/1	280						G Hobbs H. Leigh A. Kasper	7/Gas
3/5/55	11/6/55	3281	1354	250	Chg	16.640 16.560	16.460	Refit	Glass Fibre	G Hobbs W Fowell L Roberts	
26/3/56	12/5/56									Exmouth	A'boxes
8/11/56	1/12/56	3281	1354	250		16.680 16.627	16.516	Refit		G Hobbes Kilpin Kasper	
19/2/59	21/3/59	3281	1354	250		16.748 16.690	16.528	Refit		G. HOBBS A. WINDUST A. KILPIN	
28/6/60	27/8/60	3281	128/	250	Chg	16.3/5 16.790	16.605	New fitted	Idaglass	G HOBBS A KASPER L ROBERTS	GENERAL CONVERSION. AWS & Speedo Fitted.

Author's note

As stated earlier, the forgoing text and illustrations represent everything the writer has been able to glean from as many archives, museums, and private individuals as has been possible. I jokingly thought perhaps I should even have included a second subtitle along the lines of 'Well, everything I have been able to find out!' but I certainly did not want to give the impression it was a half-hearted effort, which I hope, having got thus far, you will agree. I genuinely have tried over some considerable time; I invariably have several projects 'on the go' at the same time but each time I have made a pilgrimage to a museum or archive I have also attempted to search for information on the current topic, so that it is really 'Southern Oil-Burning Engines', perhaps described as on less than 'full-heat'.

It may be unusual for a writer to state the above, but it is clear there are still gaps including images of the actual installations.

Please, if you can help fill in some of those gaps, do make contact either via the publisher or direct at editorial@thesouthernway.co.uk. We would be delighted to include follow-ups in the regular *Southern Way* series.

Bibliography

Bond, Roland C., *A Lifetime with Locomotives*, Goose and Son, 1975.

Bradley, D.L., *Locomotives of the LSWR Part 2*, RCTS.

Bradley, D.L., *Locomotives of the Southern Railway Part 2*, RCTS.

Clements, Jeremy, *The GWR Exposed: Swindon in the Days of Collett and Hawksworth*, Oxford Publishing Company, 2015.

Conversion of Locomotives from Coal to Oil Burning (eight-page pamphlet), published by *The Railway Gazette*, 1946.

Derry, Richard, *The Book of the King Arthur 4-6-0s*, Irwell Press, 2008.

Derry, Richard, *The Book of the West Country and Battle of Britain Pacifics*, Irwell Press, 2014.

Eaton, R.J., *Oil Burning Locomotive. The 'inside' Story for Enthusiasts*, Transportation Press, undated but c.1947.

Elsey, Les, *Profile of the Southern Moguls*, OPC, 1986.

Harvey, Michael G., *Fratton Locomotive Depot. A Brief History 1891 to 1967*, Tricorn Books, 2012.

Harvey, Michael G. and Rooke, Eddie, *Railway Heritage Portsmouth*, Silver Link Publishing, 1997.

Holcroft, H., *Locomotive Adventure Parts 1 and 2*, Ian Allan, 1964 and 1965.

Johnson, John, and Long, R.A., edited by R.C. Bond, *British Railways Engineering 1948–80*, MAP Publications, 1981.

Middlemas, Tom, *Stroudley and his Terriers*, Pendragon, 1995.

Nock, O.S., *The British Steam Locomotive 1925–1965, Vol. 2*, third impression Ian Allan, 1986.

Pryer, G.A., *Track Layout Diagrams of the Southern Railway and BR SR. Section 2 Southampton*.

Railways, Vol. 9, 1948.

Robertson, Kevin, *Leader and Southern Experimental Steam*, Alan Sutton Publishing, 1990.

Robertson, Kevin, *Southern Way. Special Issue No. 3: Wartime Southern: Preparation, ARP and Enemy Action*, Noodle Books, 2009.

Robertson, Kevin, *The GWR Gas Turbines – a Myth Exposed*, Alan Sutton, 1989.

Sixsmith, Ian, *The Book of the Southern Moguls*, Irwell Press, 2018.

Smith, Peter, *Somerset & Dorset from the Footplate*, Crecy Publishing, 2019 (reprint).

The Railway Magazine, The Railway Observer, The Railway Pictorial and Locomotive Review Vol. 1 for 1946, have all been referred to but in total regretfully contain little information.

What is really missing is an article in any publication entitled (or similar to) 'Experience with oil-fired locomotives (in the UK)'.

Sources

National Archives files

   AN157/219

   Rail 157/219

   Rail 1182/211

   Rail 1188/212

   Rail 1188/213

   ZSPC 11/408 R/Mag 1897

Notes from the J.G. Click archives held at the National Railway Museum.

The private notebooks and observations of the late John Bailey and the late Tony Sedgewick.

In 1952 the Institute of Locomotive Engineers published a paper by W.C. Ilkeson (followed by subsequent correspondence) on the topic of oil-firing but this takes a general worldwide look at the subject and adds nothing to the knowledge base of the Southern Railway scheme.

One YouTube film has been located. This dates from 1946 and does refer to the conversion of 1,200, although as it is from this time the actual film is only from the GWR. It does include a few frames of the oil burner itself. https://www.youtube.com/watch?v=qISLfouQJIw

Author's note

As far as the author is able to ascertain, there is little of consequence published specific to oil-burning on the SR on the worldwide web. (For the GWR visit www.greatwestern.org.uk/m_in_gwr_oil_fire.htm) A first reaction could thus be one of glee as attempting to find anything original these days that is not at least duplicated or triplicated on the web can be difficult, but it also raises two questions: firstly, is it such an obscure topic that the potential interest may be counted on fingers of one hand, or is it more simply that yours truly has pressed the wrong buttons and failed to find perhaps a mammoth tome that is literally sat there waiting?

The fact a topic is not available on the web could be for several reasons. Either nothing has been located or to those who upload items of railway interest such an item is only of very restricted interest. I have to be honest and say I somehow cannot see this work on oil-burning steam engines becoming a best-seller but having a liking for the obscure, to me that is all the more reason for recording it! (Around this time my wife happened to ask what I was currently working on. I responded accordingly. The result from her was a speechless look – it said it all. As they might say in certain places, 'I rest my case m'lud.')

(The writer has no known connection with any person having the same surname mentioned in the text.)

Index

Southern Way

The regular volume for the Southern devotee

MOST RECENT BACK ISSUES

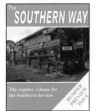 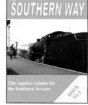 

 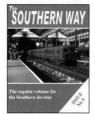  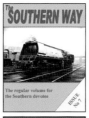   

 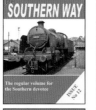 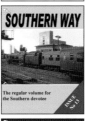 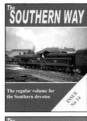   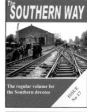

 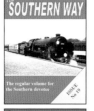 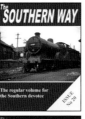    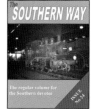

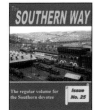  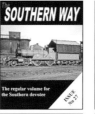   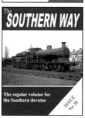 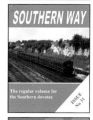

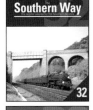 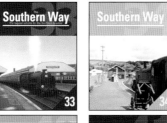  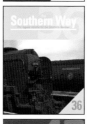  

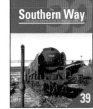   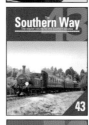 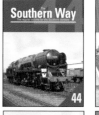 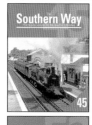

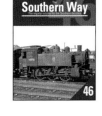  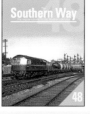  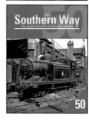 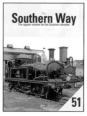 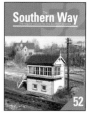

The Southern Way is available from all good book sellers, or in case of difficulty, direct from the publisher. (Post free UK) Each regular issue contains at least 96 pages including colour content.

£11.95 each
£12.95 from Issue 7
£14.50 from Issue 21
£14.95 from Issue 35

Subscription for four-issues available
(Post free in the UK)
www.crecy.co.uk

103

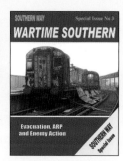
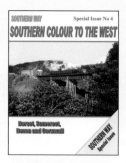
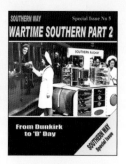

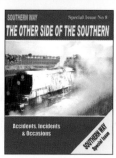
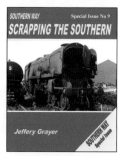
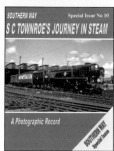
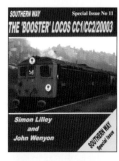
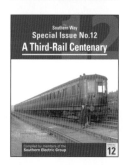
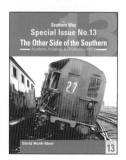